Handbook for Healing

SUPPLEMENT TO
HOW TO HEAL THE SICK

by Charles ♥ Frances Hunter

Published by HUNTER BOOKS
201 McClellan Road
Kingwood, Texas 77339

BOOKS BY CHARLES ♥ FRANCES HUNTER

A CONFESSION A DAY KEEPS THE DEVIL AWAY
ANGELS ON ASSIGNMENT
ARE YOU TIRED?
BORN AGAIN! WHAT DO YOU MEAN?
COME ALIVE
DON'T LIMIT GOD
FOLLOW ME
GOD IS FABULOUS
GOD'S ANSWER TO FAT...LOØSE IT!
GOD'S CONDITIONS FOR PROSPERITY
HANDBOOK FOR HEALING
HIS POWER THROUGH YOU
HOT LINE TO HEAVEN
HOW TO HEAL THE SICK
HOW TO MAKE YOUR MARRIAGE EXCITING
IF YOU REALLY LOVE ME...
IMPOSSIBLE MIRACLES
IT'S SO SIMPLE (formerly HANG LOOSE WITH JESUS)
LET'S GO WITNESSING (formerly GO, MAN, GO)
MEMORIZING MADE EASY
MY LOVE AFFAIR WITH CHARLES
NUGGETS OF TRUTH
POSSESSING THE MIND OF CHRIST
P.T.L.A. (Praise the Lord, Anyway!)
SIMPLE AS A.B.C.
SINCE JESUS PASSED BY
the fabulous SKINNIE MINNIE RECIPE BOOK
SUPERNATURAL HORIZONS (from Glory to Glory)
THE DEVIL WANTS YOUR MIND
THE TWO SIDES OF A COIN
THIS WAY UP!
WHY SHOULD "I" SPEAK IN TONGUES???

ISBN # O-917726-91-X

Scripture quotations are taken from:
The Living Bible, Paraphrased (TLB), ᶜ1971 by Tyndale House Publishers, Wheaton, Il.
The New King James Version (NKJV), ᵈ1979, 1980, 1982 by Thomas Nelson, Inc.,
Nashville, Tn.

TABLE OF CONTENTS

Handbook for Healing

In the event your Christian Bookstore does not have any of the books written by Charles and Frances Hunter or published by Hunter Books, please write for price list and order blank from HUNTER BOOKS. Video and audio tapes by Charles and Frances Hunter are also available.

For additional information on how to have a Video Healing School in your church or Bible study group, or how to hold Healing Explosions in or among churches in your area, write to:

HUNTER MINISTRIES
201 McClellan Road
Kingwood, Texas 77339, U.S.A

FOREWORD

We began to realize a need for additional information to help people minister healing more successfully after they had read the book HOW TO HEAL THE SICK, and studied the video/audio tapes by the same name. We discovered when they got out into the "field" to practice, it was difficult to remember all the things they had learned in a short period of time, so they needed a quick refresher course.

We felt an urging of the Spirit to write a book re-emphasizing some of the things we had said as well as adding new information. We knew it should be in the form of a handbook with diseases listed alphabetically for quick reference rather than another book on healing and made our feelings known to congregations around the nation.

How we praise God for all His people who wanted to help us get this book out because they felt the same urgency we did. We want to give our very special thanks to Betty Wiggins of Albany, Georgia, who works in the computer department for the telephone company, is the mother of four children, a Spirit-filled member of a church in Albany, but who was the first one who took a lot of time to compile and send to us a copy of her suggestions for the handbook.

Also our very special thanks to Pastor Harold L. Martin, Pastoral Care, Carpenter's Home Church in Lakeland, Florida, who put in a tremendous amount of time in compiling ideas and knowledge. They gave us the format for the book. Vester P. Thomas of their church spent hours compiling the information from the doctors' panel tapes, and her work is greatly appreciated.

Pat and Keith Hemenway of House Springs, Missouri, also sent us their thoughts and we have dipped into their storehouse and used some of their suggestions for this book.

To all the rest, our heartfelt thanks because you cared enough to want to help not only us, but the entire body of Christ with your research.

To Roy J. LeRoy, D.C. who attends all of our Healing Explosions, our thanks not only for all the contributions he has made to our meetings, but for the work which went into "fine-toothing" this book before its publication. Only heaven will reveal the rewards he will receive for all of this.

And to all of you who read this and put it into effect, our sincere thanks with a grateful heart because you have caught the vision of what God is saying to the body of Christ today.

Charles and Frances Hunter

Note: This book is subject to change as God gives us new understanding and new knowledge. This is not a book of proven science, but merely a suggestion of how to define and minister to various health problems both mental and physical.

THANK YOU
TO THE MEDICAL PROFESSION

The following doctors have contributed through their attendance and medical knowledge at our doctors' panels. Much of what we have learned has come from what they so unselfishly shared.

Other doctors have been on panels or with us at Healing Explosions whom we may have missed, and others will be with us in the future. We sincerely appreciate the credibility they add and the immense help to us and the healing teams.

Dr. Charles P. Adamo, B.A., Doctor of Chiropractic
Dr. Robert Aikman, M.D., C.M., Gynecology
Dr. Alexander, Doctor of Chiropractic
Dr. Peter Alderson, Doctor of Chiropractic
Dr. Larry Barge, M.D.
Dr. Raj Beliram, M.Sc. P.H.D., Pathology
Dr. David Bigby, M.D., Psychiatry
Dr. Paul Boegel, D.D.S., Periodontist
Dr. Dale C. Clark, Doctor of Chiropractic
Dr. Pat Crotty, Doctor of Chiropractic
Dr. Thomas Davis, M.D., Psychiatry
Dr. Michael Dunn, M.D., Surgeon
Dr. Burton Dupuy, Optometrist
Dr. Norman L. Dykes, M.D., Internal Medicine
Dr. H. Bruce Ewart, Ph.D., Counselor
Dr. W. Douglas Fowler, Jr., M.D., Surgeon
Dr. Ralph Gardner, Doctor of Chiropractic

Dr. Thomas Gorman, M.D., Ophthamology
Dr. Wayne Graves, Doctor of Osteopathy
Dr. Charles Guessner, D.D.S.
Dr. Steve Gyland, M.D., Pediatrics
Dr. Gerald Hall, Doctor of Chiropractic
Dr. David Hartz, M.D., General Practice
Dr. Richard Henderson, M.D., Psychiatrist
Dr. E.T. Hesse, Jr., Doctor of Chiropractor
Dr. Roger Hill, Optometrist
Dr. Randy Horton, Doctor of Osteopathy
Dr. Jeff Howard, Doctor of Chiropractic
Dr. Carol Hunt, M.D., Anesthesia
Dr. Paul Jacobs, D.D.S.
Dr. Richard Janson, M.D., Ophthamology
Dr. Richard Jantzen, M.D.
Dr. Joy M. Johnson, M.D., Radiology
Dr. Frank Keller, M.D., Preventative Medicine
Dr. Ben Kitchings, M.D.
Dr. Alice Lane, Homeopathy/Nutrition
Dr. Roy LeRoy, Doctor of Chiropractic
*Dr. Jonathan Lewis, M.D., F.A.C.S., Orthopedic
    Surgeon*
Dr. Caroline Love, M.D., Internal Medicine
Dr. Donald Loveleth, M.D.
Dr. Joseph C.Mantheis, Doctor of Chiropractic
Dr. Marilyn Maxwell, M.D., Internist
Dr. John H. McDonald, N.D., Doctor of Chiropractic
Dr. Alex Millhouse, Doctor of Chiropractic
Dr. Patrick E. Murray, Doctor of Chiropractic
Dr. Beulah Nichols, Ph.D.
Dr. Doran L. Nicholson, Doctor of Chiropractic
Dr. Larry Norville, M.D., Podiatrist
Dr. Larry Norup, M.D., Podiatrist
Dr. Thomas A. Owen, Doctor of Chiropractic

Dr. Suzanne M. Peoples, M.D.
Dr. Madelyn Permutt, Doctor of Chiropractic
Dr. Robert C. Pfeiler, M.D., Psychiatrist
Dr. Harrison Prater, Doctor of Chiropractic
Dr. Curt Priest, M.D., Emergency Medicine
Dr. James Price, D.D.S.
Dr. Frank Pushtarina, Doctor of Chiropractic
Dr. Daniel Reierson, Doctor of Chiropractic
Dr. Kenneth Romanoff, D.D.S.
Dr. R.J. Rozich, Doctor of Chiropractic
Dr. Ozzie Sailor, M.D., Surgeon
Dr. Steven G. Seifert, Doctor of Chiropractic
Dr. Robert Shiffman, Doctor of Chiropractic
Dr. Jeff Sitron, Doctor of Chiropractic
Dr. James R. Slusher, Doctor of Chiropractic
Dr. Gerald W Spencer, D.D.S., Orthodontics
Dr. Charles Stanback, M.D., Family Practice
Dr. Thomas Stanley, M.D., Pediatrician
Dr. Dan Strader, Nutritionist
Dr. Anthony Sunseri, D.D.S.
Dr. Mary Ruth Swope, Nutritionist
Dr. Terry Terrell, D.D.S., Periodondist
Dr. David Thompson, Doctor of Chiropractic
Dr. Michael Vanaria, Doctor of Chiropractic
Dr. Larry White, Doctor of Chiropractic
Dr. Joel Wise, Doctor of Chiropractic
Dr. James Wyllie, Doctor of Chiropractic
Gene Clark, R.N.
Georgia Cohen, R.N.
Marilyn Howe, R.N.
Ella Jansen, R.N.
Betty Mills, R.N.
Yvonne Moffit, R.N.
Bobby Smith, R.N.
Ouida Walsh, R.N.

Chapter One

The Sovereignty of God

By Frances

"Hallelujah! I want to express publicly before his people my heartfelt thanks to God for his mighty miracles. All who are thankful should ponder them with me. FOR HIS MIRACLES DEMONSTRATE HIS HONOR, MAJESTY, AND ETERNAL GOODNESS" (Ps. 111:1-4 TLB).

Praise God, we serve a God of miracles. A God who wants us to walk in the supernatural and to see miracles happen just like they did when Jesus walked on this earth — just like His disciples did.

"Jesus Christ is the same yesterday, today and forever" (Heb. 13:8 TLB).

Praise God, we serve an unchanging God. If we truly believe with our entire being that Jesus is the same yesterday, today and forever, then we will have to believe that He is going to be doing the same miracles today that He did yesterday and that He is going to be doing tomorrow. Only this time, He is going to be doing them by using the people He lives in and through.

Jesus said, *"In solemn truth I tell you, anyone believing in me shall do the same miracles I have done, and even greater ones, because I am going to be with the Father. You can ask him for anything, using my name, and I will do it, for this will bring praise to the Father because of what I, the Son, will do for you. Yes, ask anything, using my name, and I will do it!"* (John 14:12-14 TLB).

If Jesus said it, it has to be true! The believers are going to do exactly the same things He did, and even greater things! Not because of our own righteousness or power, but just because Jesus said we would.

We often use the latter part of that scripture as a regular prayer scripture, but we need to realize the conditions under which you can ask Him for anything — you must be out doing the miracles that He said we would do!

We praise God for every miracle we see, whether it is accomplished in an airport, a television station, a grocery store, an office, a service station or in church. We love to tell people about the miracles which happen because their faith is ignited for miracles to happen to them and through them! God not only wants us to be on the receiving end of miracles, but He also wants us to be on the performing end.

In Hosea 4:6, it says, *"My people are destroyed for lack of knowledge"* (NKJV).

But today, in the twentieth century, people are hungry for knowledge and are aggressively seeking it so that they can actually do the miracles and walk in the supernatural just like Jesus said we would.

At our Healing Explosions, we see evidence over and over again of how people who are trained to heal the sick are shocked that they, too, can operate in the supernatural. They look at their hands and say, "I didn't believe God could use me this way!"

Today is the hour of the believer, when God is calling ALL believers to begin to do the things He wants us to do. Christianity is not a religion of going to church on Sunday morning, getting pumped full of scripture and inspiring sermons, and then sitting on them for a week until we go back to church and listen again.

Christianity is a way of life! It is saying and doing the same things Jesus did, and walking in the same steps He did! Paul preached so powerfully, *"I have been crucified with Christ; it is no longer I who live, but Christ lives IN me; and the life which I now live in the flesh I live by faith in the Son of God, who loved me and gave Himself for me"* (Gal. 2:20 NKJV).

We need to understand with our hearts and not with our minds that Jesus Christ is actually living inside of us, wanting to manifest Himself to the world in and through us!

This is truly the hour of the believer when God is speaking to our hearts and telling us to get off of the padded, comfortable pews and get into the arena where we can begin to do the work He has called us to do.

The five-fold ministry is *"for the equipping of the saints for the work of ministry, for the edifying of the body of Christ"* (Eph. 4:12, NKJV). The five-fold ministry of the apostle, the prophet, the evangelist, the pastor, and the teacher is for getting the body of Christ taught, trained, matured, and educated in how to perform the work Jesus said we would do. Too long we have felt that the five-fold ministry was to do all the work and let the saints rest. No more; this is the hour of power and this is the hour of action when the sleeping giant is coming into its own.

No longer are we to be a weak, spineless church without power and miracles, but a powerful church walking in the super-natural at every service and every hour of every day.

We have just gone through our Bibles and circled everything in the book of Acts that has to do with the supernatural. Almost everything is circled! Why? BECAUSE THAT CHURCH IS THE PROTOTYPE OF WHAT THE CHURCH SHOULD BE TODAY.

Believers should be (and many are) going out and doing miracles in their every-day life.

During a photography session the other day, they asked us to pose. We both answered the same way at the same time: "Let us talk and tell you what we do, and then when you get the right expression, take the picture!"

Because we love to talk about Jesus and

what He is doing in the world today, we began to share some of the miracles that happen during our Healing Explosions and in our daily lives as we walk among the people!

Time came to change the film! One of the photographers stepped out and said, "I have a problem with my neck. It hurts all the time and I am in constant agony."

Glory! Here was an opportunity for Jesus! We said, "No problem," laid hands on her, did "the neck thing", and she was instantly healed!

The film was back in the camera, so we continued to share more miracles telling what God is doing today. Then came time for another film change!

Another person walked up and said as she wheezed, "I have terrible asthma, can you do anything about that?"

We said, "No problem," and bound the devil in the name of Jesus, cast out the spirit of asthma, commanded new lungs to form, and commanded the bronchial tubes to be opened along with the air sacs. Suddenly, the wheezing stopped and she was taking deep breaths.

They were ready to shoot again! Then

once again came time to change film. Another individual jumped out from the back of the studio and said, "I was in an automobile accident years ago and got a whiplash. Can you do anything about that?"

We did "the total thing" and this Jewish man was instantly healed by the power of God and the authority we have in the name of Jesus!

When we left to return to the office, Charles looked at me and said, "That was a day just like the disciples had when they were here, wasn't it?" That's the way every day should be in the life of a Christian!

The next day we went to Cleveland, Ohio to be on a television program. When we returned home, we saw a friend in the airport we had not seen for several years. He was meeting his mother who happened to be on the same plane we came in on, so he introduced us and she said, "I have a horrible fungus in my throat and I can hardly swallow. Can you help me?"

What better place to do a miracle than in a busy airport! I laid hands on her and her throat was instantly healed. Then she told us that she had just had a bladder operation and was in pain. Charles immediately did "the pelvic thing" (yes, right on the busy concourse of the airport) and "the leg thing" and she could not believe what had happened right in front of her eyes. Even her arthritic knee was healed. Her husband received the baptism with the Holy Spirit a few minutes later — also in the airport.

As we went to get our car, we were both praising God and thanking Him for demonstrating His honor, majesty and eternal goodness through the miracles we had just seen and which He had done through two people who happen to believe the Word of God is true and applicable to today!

Through the Healing Explosions we have seen many people we have trained step out in faith and believe that God wants to use them. Through the doctors' panels, we have learned many things which have been of tremendous help to us. We are now seeing a significant increase in the percentage of people healed by the power of God through the name of Jesus!

One of the most important things we need to remember at all times is that miracles can only be accomplished by the power of God's Holy Spirit and the name of Jesus. Jesus said, *"All authority has been given to*

Me in heaven and on earth" (Matt. 28:18 NKJV).

Every bit of God's authority had been given to Him, but look what He said in Luke 10:19 (NKJV): *"Behold, I give YOU the authority to trample on serpents and scorpions, and over ALL the power of the enemy, and nothing shall by any means hurt you."* He turned right around and trusted us with the power that had been given to Him! Why? So we would not be powerless, but would have the same authority He had and would perform the same miracles He did!

We cannot accept part of the Bible and then throw the rest out! If we believe He came to save us from sin and to bring us into eternal life, then we must believe the rest where he tells us to go out and do the same things He did!

Jesus said it was not by His power that He did miracles, but by the power of His Father. That same Holy Spirit has been given to us with the same unlimited power so that we can accomplish what needs to be accomplished on the earth today! Let's use it and enjoy it!

There is a very fine line in teaching people that the authority and power has been given to us to use, and yet to make sure that we take no credit for ourselves, but that we thank God and give Him all the praise and the glory for everything that is accomplished, even though we are the vessels He uses.

We can get caught up in false humility and believe that we have no ability, and yet by the same token, we can get caught up in ego and pride and take all the credit for ourselves. We need to remember that the glory for every miracle that happens belongs to God!

He has promised us that "all the earth shall be filled with the glory of God." Jesus told us in the seventeenth chapter of John that we *are* His glory. Why are we His glory? Because we are doing the things He told us to do. We cannot ever hope to be His glory unless we are fulfilling His commandments, so the earth will be filled with a people who are casting out devils, preaching the gospel, speaking in tongues, ministering the baptism, and healing the sick!

We praise God for the many doctors He has sent to be on our doctors' panels in the various Healing Explosions. We never know who is coming, but He always brings new experts from many fields of medicine. How we praise God that we have been joined by medical doctors, orthopedic surgeons, pediatricians, obstetricians, podiatrists, chiropractors, ophthalmologists, opticians, optometrists, dentists, orthodontists, nutritionists, gynecologists, osteopaths, pathologists, surgeons and other fields of medicine.

Their great medical knowledge, combined with the spiritual knowledge God gives, has brought about many healings which might not have otherwise been accomplished. Of course, remember at all times that God is sovereign and He can perform miracles any way He chooses. Many of these doctors have told us that their lives have been completely revolutionized by what they have learned by being a part of a doctors' panel and a Healing Explosion. And how we thank God for that!

Remember that we are not doctors ourselves and therefore cannot tell someone to either stop or start taking medicine. If you do, you are practicing medicine and that is illegal, unless you actually are a licensed physician. After speaking healing to a person, tell them to return to their doctor because their healing will stand up under an examination, an x-ray or a blood test! All the healings God has given us have stood the test of medical examinations.

People have asked, "Why don't you go and empty the hospitals?"

Probably the best reason we can give you is — it's not legal. When invited by someone in a hospital or by their family or friend, it is acceptable to minister in a hospital, but even then, obey hospital regulations. Don't be over-zealous and tell them to remove their tubes or to get up and walk — you would be practicing medicine. That determination must be made by their physician.

Even a Spirit-filled doctor who ministers to someone who is ill could not necessarily issue such an order. Only the patient's physician can give directions regarding their patient and their treatment. A licensed physician must have special permission from the hospital board to practice at that facility. To be a consultant or "practice" in another hospital, special permission must also be obtained. Because a doctor is licensed in one state, he does not have the right to practice medicine in another state. Just as physicians must work within rules and regulations in "healing the sick", so must we as "ministers" of Jesus' healing power operate within specific guidelines.

God will honor a faithful and a sincere heart, but we always need to remember that God also gives us common sense and tells us to obey the law at all times. We need to confine our healing techniques to those who want to be healed by God. Jesus healed all "who came to Him;" He did not heal all who were in Israel.

This book is a combination of help from many of these doctors, information taken from the doctors' panel tapes, and things we have learned — by trying more than one thing if the first one doesn't work. It is amazing how we have learned by just out-and-out persistence.

Charles as a CPA (certified public accountant) and I as the owner of a printing company had to make things work. We carried this same tenacity into the healing ministry — we continue until we find out how God wants something done. We haven't reached 100% yet; however, we will because Jesus said so!

We have done our best to put into simple terms some of the successful ways we have learned and used to minister healing to the sick. However, we want to remind you again that God is sovereign; and regardless of all the things you learn, He can still do it His way!

Just when we think we have something all figured out, God moves in an entirely different way, but whichever way He does it, we give Him all the praise and all the glory! We praise God for all the healings we have seen accomplished in the name of Jesus and by the power of God's Holy Spirit whether He does it "our" way or not!

All of these ways are not foolproof, because if they were, then we would be God! Jesus healed them ALL, and He said we would do the same things He did. So the day is coming when the BELIEVERS (that means you and me) will heal them ALL. The motto of all of our teaching is, "If Charles and Frances can do it, YOU can do it, too!" We're working toward that day when every person we touch is totally healed by the power of God working through us!

These suggestions for healing the sick have worked remarkably well for us and many other people, and we know they will also work for you. However, if you forget some of the things, just remember that with

God, ALL things are possible whether you recall all the little details or not! This book is provided only as a guide and not as a rule book. We, no doubt, will discover better, more effective ways to minister healing and so will you. We readily accept these changes so we can increase our effectiveness in ministering healing.

Please don't memorize, but rather rely on a general understanding and the leading of the Holy Spirit. These are guidelines only. These are things we have done, or realized from doctors' panels, and because they have resulted in healings, we pass them on to you.

This *Handbook for Healing* is intended as a quick review of the book *How to Heal the Sick*, the video/audio tapes by the same name, and the pre-explosion teaching sessions. WE DO NOT RECOMMEND THAT YOU ATTEMPT TO USE WHAT WE HAVE WRITTEN IN THIS BOOK UNTIL YOU HAVE READ THE BOOK "HOW TO HEAL THE SICK," OR STUDIED THE VIDEO/AUDIO TAPES BY THE SAME TITLE. This, then, is a supplement to what you have learned and can be used as a quick reference refresher course.

Don't get discouraged if you try everything, and nothing seems to work. As Paul said, *"...having done all, to stand"* (Eph. 6:13 NKJV). Remember, you have laid hands on them and the power of God has gone into them and the healing has started even though there may not be an outward man-ifestation. Let the Holy Spirit "penicillin-power" have time to work.

Just the other day a man approached me asking if I remembered praying for a little baby fourteen years ago who had no skull. Only the sides of the skull were present, the top was absent revealing just a soft mass. The parents had a helmet-like contraption on the baby's head for protection. I remem-bered ministering to the baby. When I laid hands on him, I "saw" nothing and have heard nothing from the parents since then. I would love to have seen an instant miracle where the skull bones formed immediately, but God chose not to do it that way. Having done all I knew to do, I stood!

As I recalled the incident, the man re-ported that within two months after I laid hands on that incomplete head, the baby had a perfect skull. Today, fourteen years later, he is a healthy, normal human being! Re-member, you don't always get to see your miracles! But God records them all in heaven. Glory!

I didn't learn to walk until I tried.

I didn't learn to talk until I tried.

I didn't learn to drive a car until I tried.

I didn't learn to type until I tried and kept on trying!

I didn't learn to heal the sick the first time I tried either.

I haven't learned how to heal ALL the sick, but I'm trying and I'm going to keep on trying until we see 100% of the people we lay hands on totally healed.

The desire of my heart is to see those little children who have been attacked in their mother's womb by the devil himself and who have epilepsy, mental retardation, blindness, no hearing, imperfect bodies and other deformities — totally and completely healed by the power of God when I hand them back to their parents.

I haven't seen many such instant healings of afflicted children as yet, but I'm going to keep trying and learning all I can until manifestations of total healings become a reality not only in our lives, but in yours as well.

Jesus came to seek and to save the lost

and He used healing as a tool. He wants us to do exactly the same thing. There is nothing that will convince a sinner of the reality of Jesus faster than witnessing a miracle.

One of our healing schools in Israel was contacted by a Jewish family who needed a healing miracle. They resisted the use of Jesus' name, but finally said it could be used if the healing team felt it was absolutely necessary. The man had a back problem as a result of an accident. As the healing team ministered to him in the name of Jesus, he was completely healed.

The wife had told them she had a problem with her lungs. When the healing team asked her if they could lay hands on her, she said, "When you grew out my husband's legs and his back was healed, that blue flame which came out of your hands came right across the room into my lungs. I'm healed!"

Then the husband said, "If that is Jesus, we want to accept Him as our Messiah!" They both were saved that day! A miracle is worth a million words!

For her to be allowed to see blue flames shoot across a room and into her lungs was a sovereign act of God and a sign to a Jewish couple. So regardless of how much we learn about healing the sick (and we should learn as much as possible) let us never underestimate the sovereignty of God.

He can perform miracles and healings any way He wants to!

Think On These Things
By Madeline Permutt, D.C.

"A merry heart doeth like a medicine but a broken spirit drieth the bones" (Prov. 17:22). When we laugh, when we are happy, when we praise God, when we exercise, a substance called ENDORPHINS is released in our bodies which relieves pain and is healing (acts as "medicine") to the tissues of our body. Synthetic "morphine" was patterned from endorphins. God is so good!! Amen!

And, of course, the contrary is true. If we are not joyful, if we do not praise God, if we don't exercise, the endorphins do not flow and we experience pain and sickness (and a broken spirit drieth the bones).

Chapter Two

When You Touch God

by Charles

In 1969, after totally committing my life to God, He took my spirit and soul out of my body and zoomed me into space and held me in His glorious golden light, and then returned me to my earthly body. The complete story is in our books, FOLLOW ME, PRAISE THE LORD, ANYWAY!, and BORN AGAIN, WHAT DO YOU MEAN?

As I looked at my spirit out of my body before my soul went into the spirit, my body looked identical to me — size, shape, and even the face was the same except that you could see through this spirit body as if it was carved out of a thin cloud or fog.

When God made the Bible come alive to

me, it was clear that when we are born again and baptized with the Holy Spirit, our spirits are filled with God's Holy Spirit. I realized then that my spirit, the size of me, was actually and literally filled full of the Spirit of God. I also realized that when Jesus came into my life, He lived in me and that He filled my spirit and soul with His Spirit. Paul spoke of *"Christ in you, the hope of glory...and if the Spirit of Christ is not in you, you are not a Christian* (Romans 8).

I love the way Jesus put it, and love it most in the Living Bible, *"My prayer for all of them is that they will be of one heart and mind, just as you and I are, Father — that JUST AS YOU ARE IN ME AND I AM IN YOU, SO THEY WILL BE IN US, and the world will believe you sent me"* (John 17:21 TLB).

When I touch your finger, I am touching God and Jesus; when I touch the top of your head or the bottom of your feet, I am touching God and Jesus in you.

By knowing this, I know that the power of God's Holy Spirit from within me is what heals the sick and sets the captives free. Jesus said, "I felt healing virtue go out of me." That's the power which heals the sick.

If I went to a doctor with an infection in my body, after diagnosing it, he would possibly say, "Nurse, give him two cc's of penicillin and that will kill the infectious germs." Suppose the nurse came back to the doctor holding a bottle of penicillin and the syringe needle and said, "Doctor, I don't know how to get this out of the bottle and into his body." Suppose the doctor answered, "I don't either."

Would the penicillin heal my sickness? Of course not. When our spirits are totally and completely filled with God's Holy Spirit, we still must know how to dispense this Holy Spirit "penicillin" into the bodies of the sick people to heal them. It is God's Holy Spirit power which heals, and the simple principle of healing is to dispense this power from the Spirit of God within our spirits into the bodies of the sick people.

That is one of the main things we are teaching from our book and video/audio tapes, HOW TO HEAL THE SICK, and at Healing Explosions. Once you learn that, then it is simple faith to know that God's power can and will heal anything sick which it touches.

As you study the book HOW TO HEAL

THE SICK you will see the explanations given as to how to dispense this power through laying on of hands, commanding, putting faith into action, casting out demons, and other ways Jesus and the disciples used to minister healing to the sick.

Jesus said, YOU (among other things) are to lay your hands on the sick and heal them (The Living Bible); or, and they shall recover (NKJV).

Tens of thousands of believers who have learned through our book and video/audio tapes how to dispense the power of God's Holy Spirit in Jesus' name are seeing miracles happen daily just like Peter, James, John, Paul, and the others did in the early church.

How would you like to be in a shopping mall and see a man with his arm amputated at the shoulder, and say to the people in the mall, "Gather around, I want to show you a miracle of God." Then as you made a command in Jesus' name, the arm would grow fully with hand and fingers and fingernails! That is your opportunity and responsibility to win them to Jesus by telling them how to know Him as their Savior.

How many do you think would accept Him?   ALL!

Chapter Three

Falling Under the Power

By Charles

We know from tens or hundreds of thousands on whom we have laid hands that the Holy Spirit does deep healing of spirits, sickness, injuries, depression, attitudes, habits, hurts, abuses, and other needs when they fall under the power of God. This is often referred to as being slain in the Spirit, resting in the Spirit, dormission, or falling under the power.

This happened to Paul on the road to Damascus when Jesus appeared to him; it happened to the squadron of soldiers and Judas when they came to capture Jesus; it happened to John on the Isle of Patmos (Revelation), and many other places in the Bible.

We believe that the power of the Holy Spirit which brings forth this phenomenon is the same power which heals the sick, and God's power will reach into the inner recesses of our very souls to do a work much more than could be done by all the ministry in the world. That is why we lay hands on people even after their healing has been completed. We want them to receive ministry of the Holy Spirit for all their inner needs as well as physical healings.

In our own lives, Frances had every hang up in the book concerning the baptism with the Holy Spirit when Kathryn Kuhlman called her out of an audience and laid hands on her to go under the power. God knew the need of her life and mine, and when she came up from the floor, she did not have a single objection to the baptism with the Holy Spirit and shortly after that we both received. God had met the need!

After you have ministered healing, simply lay hands on their forehead or temples and say, "Jesus, bless them!" Make sure you have a catcher behind them as you allow the power of God to touch them and minister to them. However, if they do not fall under the power, do not be concerned.

We do not recommend anyone touching or talking with someone while they are under the power, because God is doing a work, and He doesn't need your help!

Chapter Four

The Gifts of the Spirit

By Charles

Jesus said ALL believers would lay hands on the sick and they would recover. He said ALL believers would cast out devils, speak in tongues, handle the old serpent, the devil, and all his poisons, and ALL believers would minister healing to the sick.

ALL believers, if obedient to Jesus, will do all of the above things in their daily walk with God and Jesus. However, Paul said something very positive about the gifts of the Spirit.

"Now concerning spiritual gifts, brethren, I do not want you to be ignorant...Now there are diversities of gifts, but the same Spirit. There are differences of ministries,

but the same Lord. And there are diversities of activities, but it is the same God who works all in all.

"But the manifestation of the Spirit is given to each one for the profit of all: for to one is given the word of wisdom through the Spirit, to another the word of knowledge through the same Spirit, to another faith by the same Spirit, to another gifts of healing by the same Spirit, to another the working of miracles, to another prophecy, to another discerning of spirits, to another different kinds of tongues, to another the interpretation of tongues. But one and the same Spirit works all these things, distributing to each one individually as He will" (I Cor. 12:1, 4-11 NKJV).

All of us need to lay hands on the sick as Jesus said, but not all are necessarily qualified to operate in the gifts of the Spirit. The gifts of healing are entirely different from laying hands on the sick. It is a supernatural endowment of the power of God which is normally manifested in services where there are large audiences, and not generally as hands are being laid on people individually, although it can be.

Recently a young boy was sleeping

through one of our services because he was ninety-five percent deaf and could hear nothing that was being said. His mother had brought him to have hands laid on him at the end of the service, but a supernatural gift of healing was present, and suddenly the boy woke up, stood up, placed his hands over his ears and said, "Let's get out of here, Mother, it's too noisy. It's hurting my ears!"

He had been supernaturally healed by the power of God without any human ministering to him. I tested his ears at the end of the service, and even though I stood several feet in back of him and whispered, he could hear every word I said! That particular gift does not operate at all times, but is a sign and wonder and an indication of a real moving of God in a service.

Two of these gifts which are mentioned and about which we want to give you a little input are two gifts which can be invaluable in healing the sick, but can also be a dangerous tool in the hands of an unseasoned Christian. They are the word of wisdom and the word of knowledge.

Bob and Joan Barker, our son-in-law and daughter, operate mightily in these gifts, having matured greatly in this area by

opening up their spirits to hear the voice of
God. Almost all of these gifts are merely
being able to hear God and then relaying
what He said, and are powerful if used cor-
rectly. However, not ALL have these gifts.
Paul said to "one" is given this gift and to
another is given another gift, so we will not
all operate in these gifts.

Wonderful things can happen if we are
operating in the Spirit, and not in the flesh,
but terrible things can happen if we operate
in the flesh! Immature Christians have a
tendency to think in terms of what they
"want" to happen and not what God is actually saying, and can step in front of God's
plans. Sometimes it is not what we actually
"want" to happen, but something that will
bring glory or praise to us.

In attempting to operate in the word of
knowledge, we have heard unseasoned
Christians say, "God just told me that you
have cancer and are dying." The person to
whom this word has been given will be panic
stricken at the thought of having cancer.

Much harm and damage can be brought
about by an immature, careless, self-seeking
person, even though they are sincere, when
they attempt to operate in the gifts of the

Spirit.

A woman fancied herself in love with one of the singers in a group who previously traveled with us, and she told him this interesting story. "I see a spirit of death hovering over you. God told me the only way to remove it was for you to divorce your wife and marry me!"

We know this is an isolated case, but this happens often to other people. This young man was frightened and asked us if we saw a spirit of death over him. We assured him we did not, but to forget what he had heard.

By Frances

The word of knowledge is invaluable in healing, because many times people do not tell or even know the truth about what is actually wrong with them. Many years ago a woman came to our service who had not spoken in years. She had been normal up until twenty years prior to her attending one of our services. I questioned her as to whether or not there had been a sickness of some kind, a high fever, or some other physical problem, and as we stood there, God said,

"Twenty years ago she saw her husband murder another man. She did not want to testify against him, so she voluntarily lost her ability to speak."

That was a situation which required the word of wisdom along with the word of knowledge. I did not speak out and say, "God just told me you saw your husband murder another man. That's your problem!" That would have been foolishness.

When the service was over, I was talking to the pastor and casually asked him if he knew anything about this particular woman's past. He said, "Oh, yes, her husband was tried for murder years ago and that is when this happened!"

I did not reveal to the pastor what God had said to me, but he certainly confirmed what I had heard. The woman was still there so I went over, laid hands on her, and asked God to remove from her mind anything that shouldn't be there, and instantly her speech returned.

The word of knowledge had been given to me personally, and had not been given to blab to the world because along with it God gave me wisdom to know how to use that word of knowledge.

The word of knowledge can be invaluable in almost any situation where you are dealing with another person, but it should be exercised first in your church under the leadership of your pastor who knows you and your spiritual maturity. This way you can be corrected, if necessary, to help you mature in this area. If you receive a word of knowledge such as I did, ask God what to do with it, and also make sure that it is God who said it in the first place.

Years ago when I was first saved, I was ministering in Sarasota, Florida at a non-pentecostal church. I knew nothing about the gifts of the Spirit, tongues, or anything else in that realm. I was praying for people at an altar, and a man walked up to me and said, "You have the gift of healing, why don't you use it?"

I didn't say a word, because I had no idea what he was talking about. He immediately turned, walked toward the door and disappeared. I've often wondered if it was an angel, but nevertheless, I didn't tell anyone or do anything about it although I continued doing the things I had been doing up to that time. Obviously it was a word of knowledge which was a genuine one because I have seen it come true, whether it came through man or angel!

Prophecies given in the flesh but received as from God have led many good Christians astray. We are to follow after the Holy Spirit rather than a prophecy. When someone prophesies over us, we lay it on the shelf until it comes true, and then we know that person is a genuine prophet, but we never run after the prophecy in an attempt to "make" it happen. If it's of God, it will happen, if it's not, it won't. It's as simple as that.

Don't be such an "eager beaver" that you ruin someone's life with your fleshly words of knowledge or prophecy. Desire to operate in the gifts, but only under controlled situations (such as your own church) until such time as you have matured sufficiently to be able to operate in public meetings. Gifts or abilities of the Spirit are to be used to accomplish what you are to do for God at that time. These gifts are not given to all, but all believers are to minister healing.

Those operating in the various abilities or gifts of the Spirit should be mature, seasoned, Spirit-filled Christians who love God and Christ Jesus with all their hearts and who put God's desires before their own desires, and who spend much time meditating in the Word of God.

If I were a baby Christian, I would spend hours and hours meditating in the Word of God, not seeking revelation knowledge, but seeking to know God and Jesus and learning to please Them. I wouldn't trust my four-year-old granddaughter to drive a car, but as she continues to grow in the simple process of living, she will eventually become qualified to learn to drive. Until then, we're going to teach her the things that are suitable for her age. The same thing is true of a new Christian.

An old saying, but nevertheless a good one, "Don't try to run before you can walk." Little children do this, and they fall quickly, and get their knees skinned! Take all of the gifts of God according to your ability and maturity to operate in them. God will give you plenty of opportunities to use them to fulfill what He has called you to do.

And pastors, we'd rather have a little wildfire than no fire, because it's easier to put out wildfire than it is to kindle dead ashes!

Chapter Five

The Neck Thing

By Charles

We decided in the beginning of our ministry that God had made everything simple and therefore we should too, and so we have entitled all the things we do in healing in a simple manner, easy to identify and easy to remember.

Sometimes it's difficult to remember where you got the first glimmer from God concerning a method of healing, and in "the neck thing" we had to go back into our memory to recall where it began and why we started doing what we're doing.

We had a guest in our home who had a pain in his toe. I "grew out" the arms and the legs and the pain did not leave. Then I asked him what the doctor said caused the pain.

We believe in doctors and we believe if you
don't get healed by divine power, you need to
go to a doctor to find out what the problem
is. Then we can know where and how to
minister healing by God's power and then it
will be easy to get healed supernaturally.

He said the chiropractor had advised
him that he had a thin disc in his back and
even though it was in the lower back, he adjusted his neck, and the pain left, although it
subsequently returned.

I put my two hands on his neck, placing
my fingers on his upper spinal column.
(*"Those who believe shall lay hands on the
sick"* (Mark 16:18 NKJV). At the same time, I
did not realize where the other parts of my
hands actually were resting. Later I discovered that the palms of my hands were on the
carotid artery, which is the main artery on
both sides of the neck, through which blood
is pumped into the brain. Therefore, this is
also applying the power of God to any part of
the brain that might need attention. The
palms were also on the nerves which go from
the brain down the front of your body.

This automatically makes your thumbs
fall right on the temporomandibular joint
which is where we have problems with what

is better known as "TMJ". You are laying hands (thumbs) on the strongest muscle of the body. Was it accidental that God made our hands so that when we placed them in the right position we would be "laying hands" on three vital parts of the body at one time? Or did He plan it so that when we started probing into how to heal the sick the supernatural way, we would discover what He knew all along?

I then, with my hands gently in place as described above, asked him to slowly turn his face to the left and then the right, then backward and forward. At the same time I was doing what we later called "the neck thing" (TNT), I commanded all the muscles, ligaments, tendons, and vertebrae to go into place and the thin disc to be healed in the name of Jesus.

Then he himself rotated his head and shouted, "The pain is gone!"

We did this for years and also discovered the results were phenomenal for headaches as well, and then one day Dr. Roy J. LeRoy, a well-known chiropractor, told us actually what we were doing and why the results were so tremendous.

We have seen outstanding healings through "the neck thing", not only in our ministry, but through the tens or hundreds of thousands whom we have taught this supernatural-natural application of God's healing power.

Almost 100% of neck problems, headaches, nerve deafness, arthritis in the neck, fractured vertebrae, deteriorated, herniated, disintegrated discs, even broken necks, and TMJ have been healed by this application of God's healing power.

You will discover that large percentages of health problems will be healed through the basic healing application of "the total thing" (TTT); growing out arms and legs, "the neck thing," (TNT) and "the pelvic thing" (TPT). This not only affects the spinal system, but affects internal parts because of nerves making muscles work properly.

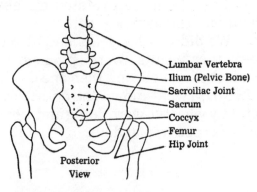

Lumbar Vertebra
Ilium (Pelvic Bone)
Sacroiliac Joint
Sacrum
Coccyx
Femur
Hip Joint

Posterior View

See Footnote on opposite page.

Chapter Six

The Pelvic Thing

By Frances

God will give you "witty inventions" and ideas beyond your ability and capability if you will be sensitive to the Holy Spirit and move when He moves!

At a service in Jacksonville, Florida, a man came up who had "duck" feet. I certainly didn't know what to pray except to command his feet to turn inward instead of outward, when a thought filtered into my mind. It was a real "flash" thought, but I knew that God had said something to me and it seemed to me as if He was indicating it had something to do with the spine.

A chiropractor was with us, so I asked him if there was a problem in the spine

Footnote: The Pelvic Thing

The sacroiliac can assume many different positions. Sometimes the ilium (pelvic bone) rotates on the sacrum and causes one leg to appear short; or it can go out of position and the legs will appear even length and still the spine is crooked (scoliosis). The sacrum can tilt forward and cause lordosis (swayback) or backward and cause a straight or "military" back. In all these examples, do the pelvic thing and command the sacrum to move into the correct position.

which caused this to happen and make the man's feet turn out.

He replied, "His pelvic bones are turned out and need to be turned inward." In the natural or chiropractic world, this would be difficult or impossible to do, but in God's kingdom and in the supernatural world, this is easy to do.

I placed my hands on the top of his pelvic bones and commanded the pelvis to rotate "in" until the feet were normal. I was probably the most surprised person there when I noticed the entire pelvic area began to turn from side to side.

I wasn't doing it!

He wasn't doing it!

It had to be the power of God!

Just as quickly as the rotating had started, it stopped, and the man fell under the power of God. When he stood up again, his feet were no longer in a "duck" position, but were perfectly straight!

Once again, God had opened a natural-supernatural channel for us to learn more about healing.

It didn't take us long to figure out that if rotating "in" with the power of God would correct "duck" feet, then surely rotating "out" would correct people with pigeon toes! We tried it, and it worked. We have seen many people since that time healed of feet that turn in!

We discussed this with many doctors on our doctors' panels and they all agreed it could be invaluable in many other diseases as well. Because of the involvement of the entire pelvic area, many female problems are healed through this simple laying on of hands. We have had hundreds of women healed of PMS (Pre-menstrual syndrome) by this simple act of commanding the female organs to go into place while the pelvis is rotating.

Many problems in the lower lumbar area (the lower five vertebrae) and the sacrum are healed through this method. Command the vertebrae to be adjusted properly. Often a frozen or dislocated sacrum is restored to its right position by doing "the pelvic thing."

Prostate problems can be healed this way by commanding the prostate to become normal.

Colon problems are healed by commanding nerves controlling the colon to become normal.

Actually, any organ or part of the body which lies between the waistline and the hips many times can be healed by this simple act.

It never hurts to look at a picture of the human body so you will know where certain parts are located. The pelvic bones are sometimes called the "hip" bones. They are the flat bones which make up your skeletal structure for the hip and pelvis area. If you will run your hands down your side in the area of your waist, you will discover the top of the bones lay right in that area, and that is where you place your fingers.

When you begin to make commands, if that portion of the body needs adjusting, the pelvis will rotate or move in one direction or the other. If nothing is needed, nothing will happen and it will not move.

Many times one side will be higher than the other, so command the high side to lower and the low side to come up. It's fabulous what the power of God can and will do!

Don't underestimate the value of this simple healing process. It is incredible what happens!

Chapter Seven

When Ministering Healing

By Charles and Frances

This HANDBOOK FOR HEALING along with the book and video/audio tapes HOW TO HEAL THE SICK can only briefly and simply teach basic principles of healing. In no sense is this to be considered all-inclusive nor to indicate any application of medical or scientific procedures or practices. These are only suggested guidelines.

We urge everyone who possibly can to attend our live pre-explosion teaching and review sessions plus the doctors' panels. Much is learned and the principles of these applications of the healing methods outlined in the Bible and our teachings are imprinted on their minds. Audio tapes of the various Healing Explosion doctors' panels are available through our office and are very valuable teachings.

If you desire further information about various diseases, many good medical dictionaries and handbooks are available through bookstores. If in doubt, ask your doctor to help you.

We can never repeat often enough that you follow the advice of your doctor. We are not doctors and we urge all believers we teach to never try to follow medical procedures, but simply to do the child-like application of God's Power in Jesus' name.

AIDS
Acquired Immune Deficiency Syndrome

A word about AIDS - Acquired Immune Deficiency Syndrome. This particular disease is presented in detail since it is such a devastating problem, and because the incidence is rapidly on the rise in our day and time. We are told that as of April, 1987, there was no medical cure for AIDS, no prospective cure, and little hope for an effective vaccine. It is apparent that the Christian community is going to see more and more people requesting ministering of healing for this disease in the immediate future.

What it is: This is a disease caused by a

virus called HTLV-III, or the AIDS virus.

What it does: The AIDS virus causes a severe reduction and depletion of the immune system of a person until their body can no longer effectively fight off infection.

How the virus is transmitted: The primary way that the AIDS virus is passed from one person to another is through sexual intercourse. It was first thought that only homosexual contact was transmitting the disease, but now it is becoming clear that people with multiple heterosexual contacts are also at risk. This obviously means that the person married to someone with AIDS is at risk of developing the disease as well.

AIDS can also be passed through blood transfusions, and through the use of dirty hypodermic needles. It could possibly also be passed from an open sore or bleeding cut into an open cut or mucous membrane of another person. There is suspicion, but no evidence, that intense kissing may transfer the virus. There is no evidence that any casual contact, like shaking hands, or a kiss on the cheek, or sneezing or coughing can infect others, but more thorough testing is needed.

How to minister to someone with AIDS:

If the person contracted the disease through either homosexual or promiscuous activity, the first thing they need to do is repent and be born again. We firmly believe there will never be a healing of AIDS without complete and genuine repentance and a turning away from the lifestyle in which they have previously been engaged.

The plan of salvation is extremely important in the healing of this particular disease so don't rush over this part of the healing.

Then rebuke and take authority over the infection in the name of Jesus, and cast out the spirit of AIDS in Jesus' name. Command healing or restoration to the entire immune system in the name of Jesus. Command the entire body to be healed and restored to normal in the name of Jesus.

The source or seed or root cause of AIDS still seems to stem from sins which are abominations to God. An innocent spouse or individual may get AIDS and not be guilty of sin themselves but the source still seems to stem from the sin.

Here are a few scriptures which clearly tell what God thinks about this sin against the body which is intended to be His temple:

All of Leviticus chapter 18 deals with the laws of sexual morality, and specifically verses 22, 24, 29 (NKJV) say, *"You shall not lie with a male as with a woman. It is an abomination...Do not defile yourselves with any of these things...For whoever commits any of these abominations, the persons who commit them shall be cut off from among their people."*

"If a man lies with a male as he lies with a woman, both of them have committed an abomination. They shall surely be put to death. Their blood shall be upon them" (Lev. 20:13 NKJV).

"Do you not know that the unrighteous will not inherit the kingdom of God? Do not be deceived. Neither fornicators nor idolaters, nor adulterers, nor homosexuals, nor sodomites, nor thieves, nor covetous, nor drunkards, nor revilers, nor extortioners will inherit the kingdom of God. And such were some of you. But you were washed, but you were sanctified, but you were justified in the name of the Lord Jesus and by the Spirit of our God" (1 Cor. 6:9-11 NKJV).

Praise God for the redemption plan of Jesus!

Is there hope for healing people with

AIDS?
    Yes — in Jesus!

MINISTERING TO CHILDREN

When ministering to children, remember that you are much bigger than they
are, and if you are not careful, you may
frighten them and lose their confidence.

This principle also applies to adults,
especially to those who have never been ex-
posed to divine healing or deliverance. Be
careful to approach them in gentleness and
love. You may be "full grown" in the supernatural, but they may be as little children
and you may frighten them and lose their
confidence.

One of the best ways to approach a child
is to come down to their level by kneeling. It
helps a great deal to always smile and talk to
them quietly and confidently. One good way
to gain contact with a youngster is to extend
your hands to them, palms upward and
open, so they can place their hands in yours.

While ministering to them, do not raise
your voice. It is possible to continue smiling
at the youngster at the same time you are

taking authority over an evil spirit and casting it out in Jesus' name. Speak with authority and that spirit will recognize that you mean business, and it will obey. A child will always recognize when someone is ministering in love, and they will respond. Therefore project to them from the inside of you that you love them and you are there to help them.

MENTAL ILLNESS

How an individual thinks is a result of what they have allowed into their mind. Therefore, when the wrong thoughts and thought patterns come across the mind, regardless of their origin, it is up to each individual to either receive, reject or replace them with the right thinking and thought pattern.

It has been said that practically all mental illness is the result of guilt. If so, that simply means there is sin in the life. To gain control and mastery of that area requires an acknowledgement by them of the problem source, a genuine repentance, with a turning away from sin, and an acceptance of Jesus Christ as Lord and Savior.

Insanity is not classified as mental illness as we discuss it here.

To minister healing, first bind and cast out the spirit of whatever the problem is: depression, oppression, schizophrenia, mania, etc. by the power of the Holy Spirit, in Jesus' name. Next speak the peace of God into that mind and heart in the name of Jesus.

Since a major part of the problem originated in wrong thinking, then the most important step is to change the thinking by renewing the mind (Romans 12:1,2) by filling the mind and the life with the Word of God. The Word says, *"Let this mind be in you which was also in Christ Jesus"* (Phil. 2:5 NKJV).

Notice that it is a choice that we must make; God will not do it for us. We are to renew our minds with God's Word by reading it, meditating on it, confessing it, occupying our minds with it, and living it, until we begin to think the same way God thinks.

Get them delivered, saved, baptized in the Holy Spirit, and into the Word of God.

Then, the only way to remain free of this bondage is to obey Jesus and be doers of the Word. That means to put the desires and purposes of God and Jesus above their own.

Those who look inward will perish in darkness, but those whose light shines outward to reveal Jesus will remain free.

"Therefore if the Son makes you free, you shall be free indeed" (John 8:36 NKJV).

SUICIDE

These people really need help, and it is best to realize that while some of them need deliverance from demonic powers, others are caught in deep feelings of defeat and depression. Tell them that God loves them and He wants them to be free if they will just ask Jesus to forgive them and to come into their heart.

In a firm but quiet voice, with power and authority, look into their eyes and cast out the spirit: "Devil, I bind you in the name of Jesus and by the power of the Holy Spirit, and I command you, spirit of suicide, to come out of them now in Jesus' name."

Minister salvation and the baptism with the Holy Spirit to give them power to live victoriously.

Urge them to get into a good church under the ministry of Spirit-filled pastors. They need to learn how to look outward and help others for only as we give can we receive.

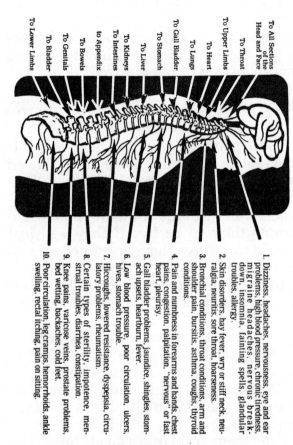

To All Sections of the Head and Face
To Throat
To Upper Limbs
To Heart
To Lungs
To Gall Bladder
To Stomach
To Liver
To Kidneys
To Intestines
to Appendix
To Bowels
To Genitals
To Bladder
To Lower Limbs

1. Dizziness, headaches, nervousness, eye and ear problems, high blood pressure, chronic tiredness, migraine headaches, nervous break-down, insomnia, fainting spells, glandular troubles, allergy.

2. Skin disorders, hay fever, wry or stiff neck, neuralgia, neuritis, sore throat, hoarseness.

3. Bronchial conditions, throat conditions, arm and shoulder pain, bursitis, asthma, coughs, thyroid conditions.

4. Pain and numbness in forearms and hands, chest pains, congestion, palpitation, "nervous" or fast heart, pleurisy.

5. Gall bladder problems, jaundice, shingles, stomach upsets, heartburn, fever.

6. Low blood pressure, poor circulation, ulcers, hives, stomach trouble.

7. Hiccoughs, lowered resistance, dyspepsia, circulatory problems, rheumatism.

8. Certain types of sterility, impotence, menstrual troubles, diarrhea, constipation.

9. Knee pains, varicose veins, prostate problems, bed wetting, backaches, cold feet.

10. Poor circulation, leg cramps, hemorrhoids, ankle swelling, rectal itching, pain on sitting.

On the right are listed a few of the many problems, disorders, and diseases which "pinched nerves can cause in the various areas of the body.

The arrows on the left point to the locations in the spine where nerves pass through very small openings on their way to and from the brain to control all the various parts and organs of the body. About 300,000 nerve fibers pass through each of 62 little openings. Just a slight dislocation of a bone (vertebra) in the spine can close one of these tiny openings enough to "pinch" a nerve and interfere with normal passage of nerve impulses.

Chapter Eight

The Spine

By
Dr. Roy J. LeRoy

Dr. Roy J. LeRoy has been at all of our Healing Explosions. He is an outstanding chiropractor who actively practiced in his field for 40 years before he retired. Now he shares his valuable knowledge and experience with us on the doctors' panels at Healing Explosions.

Norma Jean Van Dell, about whom we wrote the book IMPOSSIBLE MIRACLES, was widowed, but God sent a widower to sweep her off her feet, and she became Mrs. LeRoy in 1984. Their joint ministry to the sick is entitled IMPOSSIBLE MIRACLES MINISTRY, and is a powerful, unique ministry.

Recently something Doc said triggered a great response in us. We feel it will be a real blessing to you.

"All bitterness and resentment starts first with anger. Somebody does something to you which makes you mad. This causes an overabundance of adrenalin to be supplied into your body. The body cannot absorb the excess amount of adrenalin that shoots out, and as a result it goes into the kidneys but they are unable to carry off this excess. It has to go someplace, so it settles in the joints of the body which causes arthritis."

We would wholeheartedly recommend to anybody who has arthritis that you look deeply in your life and see if you have bitterness and unforgiveness toward another person. If so, get it out of your system.

This is not the only cause of arthritis according to statistics, but is one of the most significant.

Charles and Frances:

Dr. LeRoy has blessed our healing teams mightily in his knowledge of the spine and he has provided the following for your benefit.

THE SPINE

It is estimated that close to 85% of adults will have back and/or neck problems of some sort during their lifetime. Most of these problems are a result of some kind of injury. Usually the condition that occurs is a combination of misaligned vertebrae, muscle strain, ligament and tendon strain or tearing. In addition, the disc that sits between the vertebrae may also be damaged.

With this high an incidence of spinal problems, a large percentage of people who come for healing will have this as their complaint. Charles and Frances have given nicknames to these ways of ministering healing. These problems are almost all ministered to by:

"Growing out arms."

"Growing out legs."

"The neck thing" (TNT), and/or

"The pelvic thing" (TPT).

They call the combination of all of these "The total thing" (TTT).

Therefore we will briefly review the spine and its problems.

The vertebrae are the bones that make

up the spinal column, sitting one on top of the other. In between these vertebrae are the discs, or pads, that allow a certain amount of motion in bending and twisting the back and neck. All of these bones are held in place by sets of ligaments, tendons, and muscles. In the back the vertebral column is a channel made up of the circular rings of bone on the back of the vertebrae which house and protect the spinal cord, the main bundle of nerves running from the brain to all the parts of the body.

A severe fracture or dislocation can cause damage to the cord itself, or to any of the thirty-one pairs of nerve roots that come out from between the individual vertebrae. Damage to a disc, the pad between the vertebrae, can cause it to bulge out and put pressure on a nerve root, causing pain and at times weakness on either one side or both sides of the body.

The spine starts just under the base of the skull with what is called the cervical spine. This is the series of the first seven vertebrae, the topmost being the Atlas and the second one the Axis. The head rotates from side to side on the Atlas, and forward and backward on the Axis.

The nerves from the cervical spine supply the face and head, the neck, shoulders and partway down the arms. Any pressure on these nerves will cause pain and interference with normal function in these areas. For healing in this area we do "the neck thing."

The thoracic (or dorsal) spine consists of the next twelve vertebrae, each of which has a pair of ribs coming off the sides, forming the rib cage. The nerves that come out from the spinal cord at this level supply the lower arms, the hands, and the chest. For healing in this area, we do what is called "growing out arms."

The lumbar spine consists of the bottom five vertebrae, where the nerves supplying the legs and feet come from between the vertebrae. For healing in this area we do what is called "growing out legs."

The next bone, rather larger than the vertebrae is called the sacrum, and supplies support for the entire spinal column. This bone is also joined to the two hip, or iliac bones (a part of the pelvis) through a series of ligaments, tendons and the sacroiliac joints. For ministering healing to the entire pelvic area, we do what is called "the pelvic thing." The thigh bones, or femurs, are joined to the hip bones.

Just below the sacrum is the coccyx bone, a short bone that comes close to the rectum, also known as the tail bone.

While ministering to someone with a neck or back injury, it is not uncommon to find that they have been to a doctor, and may be wearing an orthopedic collar or brace. Do not remove or readjust the apparatus when ministering since this could be considered practicing medicine. After the person has been ministered to, we suggest that you ask them if the pain is gone. Normally they can tell whether there has been improvement while the collar or brace is still in place. If they report that the problem has improved, you may ask them if THEY want to remove the apparatus to see what God has done. Let it be their choice.

Encourage the person to return to their doctor for evaluation, qualification or verification as appropriate.

Chapter Nine

The "Appestat"

Dr. Mary Ruth Swope

Healing of the "Appestat"

Dr. Mary Ruth Swope of Melbourne, Florida, received her B.S. degree from Winthrop College in Rockville, S.C.

She then went on to receive her Master of Science degree, including nutrition, from the University of North Carolina at Greensboro.

Her doctorate is from the Columbia University in New York City.

She taught high school for seven years, then worked as a nutritionist for the Ohio Health Department for three years.

Dr. Swope then entered the college

arena where she was a member of the Foods and Nutrition Faculty at Purdue University, and later served as Head of Foods and Nutrition at the University of Nevada.

For eighteen years prior to her retirement in December, 1980, Dr. Swope was Dean of the School of Home Economics, Eastern Illinois University, Charleston, Illinois.

Well qualified in the field of nutrition, Dr. Mary Ruth Swope has made excellent contributions to the Healing Explosions. She has attended almost every Healing Explosion and her advice is excellent and up-to-date.

She is a specialist in the area of the "appestat" as she calls it, and shares some of her wealth of knowledge in this area on the following pages.

DEFINITION OF "APPESTAT"

The appestat is the appetite control center in the hypothalmus gland in the brain. It is regulated by the blood sugar level. Compare it to the thermostat in your house. When the air cools off, the furnace comes on until the temperature cuts off the thermostat. That's the way the appestat works, except that our junk-food and high-sugar diet has "broken" the appestat. God needs to repair it by readjusting the set-point. God uses you to do that by the laying on of hands and by your command.

SPIRITUAL ASPECTS OF THE OBESITY PROBLEM

Fat people are often harrassed by the following:
1. Addiction to sugar, fats, salt, junk foods, etc.
2. Gluttony
3. Caffeine
4. Craving for unwholesome drinks (ale, beer, bourbon, brandy, champagne, soft-drinks, wine, etc.)
5. Craving for unwholesome foods (pork, shrimp, catfish, etc.)
6. Morbid hunger--hunger experienced shortly after a meal which results in bulimia.
7. Inheritance bonds.
8. Deception of overeating (lust for food)
9. Anxiety or insecurity.
10. Fear of not getting enough to eat in the

presence of plenty.

God has promised to guide you, even in the details of situations. He knows what you need to do and say. You may not! Trust Him to act on your behalf and that of the people who are to receive deliverance and healing.

When praying for people, put one hand on their forehead. God will become their nutrition teacher and will show them what to eat and not to eat. Lay your other hand on their appestat at the base of their brain. God will reset their "out-of-control" appestats. They will glorify God through controlled body weight, if they obey Him.

Miracle after miracle will take place before your eyes. God's Spirit will be working in marvelous and miraculous ways.

Pray much for obese people. I will show you that is what they need. Healing of the appetite is no different than healing a kneecap or some other dysfunctioning part of the body. Illness to any part, no matter how small or inconsequential it seems, can destroy the whole being. Appetite is no exception.

Divine healing of the appestat will bring normalcy to the dietary pattern, and when eating habits return to normal, bodies heal themselves to a great extent.

Overnutrition of the body is often accompanied by undernutrition of the spirit and soul. People get fat, bloated, and often forget their God as the Israelites did! Science cannot solve this problem. That's obvious. But God can! Jesus will set the captives free through the laying on of hands.

Almost nobody in Christendom has had the vision of the devil's sneaky plan to destroy health, wealth, and happiness through diet manipulation. That is why Christians are overeating, overfed, and overweight. MILLIONS are headed for beds of affliction accompanied by high medical bills. They have not stopped to think how this affects God's marching army, His supply of soldiers, in these last days.

See obesity as a destroyer, a killer. Gluttony maims! Millions will attest to this fact. Abnormal excesses result in specific diseases that destroy the body, the soul, and the spirit. See yourself as a partial answer to this problem.

Speak to the person to whom you are ministering, without condemnation, and ask them to pray with you.

SUGGESTED PRAYER

"In the name of Jesus, I speak to my body and command my thoughts about food to line up with good nutrition. I bind any spirit of lust for sugar, fat, pork, blood, too much meat, junk foods, and all other unhealthful foods.

"I speak to my body and command my metabolism to become perfectly normal — digestive organs, I command you to work as they were meant to work, in the name of Jesus.

"I speak to my 'appestat' and command it to be healed at the upper limits, in the name of Jesus. I will no longer experience a ferocious appetite or be tempted to go on eating binges.

"I say, appetite, that you will learn to love pleasant bread and you will eat it willingly, without murmuring — for the Glory of God and the sake of the Kingdom, in the name of Jesus." Amen.

"For God is at work within you, helping you want to obey him, and then helping you do what he wants" (Phil. 2:13 TLB)

SUGAR - THE INFLICTOR OF GREAT GREAT PUNISHMENT

A noted doctor said, "Sugar is the greatest scourge (a whip that inflicts great punishment) that has ever been visited on man in the name of food." He believes that it should be outlawed as a poison because that's what it is. It has perverted our appetites and ruined our internal organs. It is supplying the perfect food for our cancer, heart trouble, diabetes, soft bones, pancreatitis, kidney disease, liver disease, sticky blood platelets, dental caries, and increases our desire for coffee and alcohol. He suggests that when you substitute dextrose and any other kind of sugar for white table sugar, it is comparable to exchanging a rattlesnake for a cobra as a bed partner!

Endocrinologists agree that sugar destroys God's relative balance of the glands and nervous system. These are the glands which produce and secrete hormones into the blood or lymph, to all parts of the body.

Sugar upsets the balance and produces a hyper-secretion of hormones comparable to what you get with taking drugs and artificial hormones. In addition, it is addictive.

One of the most damaging things is that it causes the appetite control center to go helter-skelter. Sugar is devoid of any nutritional value (except calories), so the cells do not get the vitamins, minerals, enzymes, protein, etc. that they need.

When you ingest sugar, the "sugar glands" go to work telling you to eat more food so that your cells might have a chance to get the missing nutrients for which they are looking. Your pancreas works harder to provide more insulin. It tells your brain to have you eat more sugar because it cannot slow down fast enough to keep from throwing you into a coma. So, you receive double damage — you eat more junk and your glands keep working to tell you to give them more nutrients!

A recent study in which people ate 1,800 calories per day of sweet foods, reported up to a 40% increase in cholesterol in two weeks. The most frightening finding was that table sugar was found in the urine of all participants.

As one doctor said, "It remains to be seen what the 21st century people will be like; their endocrine glands are going to be damaged from birth. Heart disease will be up, even from birth; we are seeing children born now with plugged blood vessels, especially boy babies.

WHO WILL PROTECT US FROM THIS DESTRUCTION?

Will dieticians? No, they give you jello, which has 60% sugar in it, right after you've been assaulted by a surgeon's knife!

Will home economics teachers? No, they are still teaching young people to bake the richest, sweetest cookies, cakes, puddings, etc. that you can imagine.

Will food manufacturers? No, sugar is cheap and sugar sells products. So, they will find new ways to foist more sugar on us. Filled, iced, and fried doughnuts will attest to that!

A noted doctor says that we are headed for nutritional obliteration. The devil loves it! God hates it! It was never His plan for man to destroy himself through poor nutrition.

GOD'S ANSWER: HONEY

Prov. 24:13 (NKJV) - *"My son, eat honey because it is good, and the honeycomb which is sweet to your taste."*

Prov. 25:27 (NKJV) - *"It is not good to eat much honey; so to seek one's own glory is not glory."*

1. Contains at least 15 nutrients; an excellent food.
2. In raw state, is an aid to digestion because of enzyme content.
3. In moderation, does not adversely affect immune system.
4. A natural antibiotic.

5. Satisfies appetite; does not interfere with desire for nourishing food.
6. In moderation, does not contribute to weight gain.
7. Enters bloodstream slowly and perfectly (2 calories per minute).
8. In moderation, is not harmful to the joints.
9. Useful to alcoholics when recovering.
10. Is psychologically and emotionally satisfying.
11. Does not destroy bone structure.

SATAN'S COUNTERFEIT: SUGAR

Jer. 6:20 (NKJV) - *"For what purpose to me comes...sweet cane from a far country."*

1. No nutrients. A POISON. Not a food.
2. Sugar in the stomach causes fermentation and putrefication and interferes with digestion.
3. Completely breaks down immune system causing many disease conditions to flourish.
4. Causes fermentation leading to bacterial growth and many diseases.
5. Causes gluttony and craving for more sweets.
6. One of the main causes of excess weight.
7. Produces a yo-yo effect.

8. Contributes to arthritis.

9. Excess sugar contributes to alcoholism.
10. Causes mental disturbances, nervous disorders and stress.
11. Causes calcium leakage from bones, resulting in osteoporosis.

GOD'S ANSWER: HONEY   *SATAN'S COUNTERFEIT:*
SUGAR

12. Does not contribute to heart disease (attack/strokes) or high-blood pressure.
13. Does not cause distortion of vision.

12. Causes heart disease and high-blood pressure.

13. Dims and blurs vision and can cause double vision (your eyes are what you eat).

THE BOTTOM LINE:

Sugar contributes to a diseased state of health and often results in shortened lifespan.

Chapter Ten

Eye Healings

Dr. Burton J. Dupuy, Jr.

Dr. Burton J. Dupuy Jr., an optometrist from Natchitoches, Louisiana, attended the New Orleans healing seminar, and the information he shared with us resulted in more eye healings than in all of our other Healing Explosions put together. The results continue, so we pass this information on to you.

Dr. Dupuy:

There are two eye problems which you will probably run into most often. They are glaucoma and cataracts.

Some people say these eye problems are inherited. You might ask the person if anyone in their family has one of these diseases or situations. They are not necessarily inherited.

Cataracts are due to poor circulation, I believe, more than anything else. We're not really sure what causes it, but we do know that a lack of oxygen supply to the lens in the eye will cause cataracts. Some are spots, some are streaks, some are like dust on the cornea, some are just milky so there are all types. Pray that the spot in the eye will be removed. Command the spirit of inheritance to come out.

A cataract is not a growth. The lens in the eye where the cataract is formed is shaped like a magnifying lens. It is thick in the middle and thin on the edges. It is composed of layer after layer of skin, similar to an onion. What happens is these layers start drying out in different areas and this causes a spot. So when the light comes through, when we look into the eye, we see a black spot in there. It is not a growth, it is not cancerous. It is just a change or drying out of the tissue. Pray that the tissue be restored to normal and the blood supply to the eye be replenished.

Glaucoma is an increase of pressure in

the eye. The fluids in the eye are constantly being replaced and drained out. The canals are slim around the outer area of the iris where the fluids drain out of the eye, and if these canals become clogged, then the drainage slows down and the pressure builds up. It's like blowing air into a balloon. Command the canals to be opened, command the spirit of inheritance to come out, and command the pressure to be relieved and go down to normal, in Jesus' name.

Chapter Eleven

Don't Forget

By
Charles and Frances

1. Ask the person to whom you are ministering what their problem is; what does their doctor say is wrong.
2. It is not important to know all the medical details of an illness to be able to minister healing. It is important to know what the problem is, and address the problem itself, rather than the symptoms. Above all, remember to be practical, which means to listen carefully to what the person is saying so that you minister healing to the specific problem.
3. When you ask someone what their dis-

ease is, say "That's easy" after their answer regardless of how difficult their condition may sound. Remember the most fatal disease is "easy" when God steps in. We have discovered this reply gives hope to the one to whom you are ministering, and also increases your faith to hear yourself tell someone their problem is "easy."

4. Once you have ministered healing, have them put their faith into action. If their back was hurting, have them bend their back. If the problem was in their elbow, have them bend the elbow. If the problem was arthritis in the shoulder or knees, have them either swing the arm or move the leg and knee area.

5. Make sure they say, "Thank you, Jesus!" Thanksgiving to God can complete an incomplete healing.

6. Learn to look at the ones who ARE healed. If you look at the ones who are not healed your faith will tend to waver, so continue looking only at the ones who are healed and watch the percentage grow!

7. People will say, "It still hurts," and when you ask them how much of the

pain is gone, they will say, "95%, but there's still a little bit left." Encourage them to thank God for the 95% that's gone, because often when they do, the last five per cent will be manifested. We have also discovered that if they emphasize the negative, the 95% will drop to 90% and will continue to go down. Thanking Jesus is one of the best ways to get a healing completed! And by the same token, being negative can cause the 5% of the pain to increase to 10% and then to 15%, then 50% until an individual has all the pain back and has totally lost their healing.

8. Look for the absence of pain, not the pain! Look for the healing, not the sickness!

9. You are not a doctor, so don't try to practice medicine. Do not prescribe, nor recommend that people go off of their medication.

10. Do not make a diagnosis. Let the individual to whom you are ministering tell you what their problem and symptoms are.

11. Whenever you cast out a spirit, do it "In the name of Jesus and by the power of

God's Holy Spirit."

12. Remember there are two things necessary for healing to be accomplished:
The name of Jesus (Say it over and over again. You can't say it too much!)
The power of God's Holy Spirit.

13. If one thing doesn't work, ask God what to do; keep trying different things and be persistent.

14. If after ministering to the individual the best you know how, there are still no visible results, then encourage them to believe the healing has started because the healing power of God has gone into them. It's amazing how many discover later they were healed.

15. Never do anything half-heartedly for the Lord.

16. When in doubt, cast it out!

17. When in doubt, grow it out!

18. After you have ministered healing to more than one thing, you will find it helpful to go through "the arm thing" and "the leg thing" again after ministering in other areas.

19. Be particularly cautious that you have someone standing behind a person to catch them if they go under the power,

before you lay hands on them to minister. Hold them by the shoulders if there is no catcher available. If a person does not fall under the power, don't be concerned. Some do, some do not! But people get healed either way!

20. Remember you are not a physician, a chiropractor or an osteopath, and are not making adjustments, but applying the supernatural power of God.

21. Walk in boldness. Don't let fear stop you. Speak with authority. That doesn't mean speak loudly, but when you mean what you say, say it like you mean it.

22. A force field of power comes out of you. The closer you are to the person, the more power they will feel and receive. Stand close but in good taste.

23. Concentrate on one of their problems at a time when you minister healing; don't minister to all the physical problems in the same sentence. Do one at a time. Check to see how the first condition is progressing before going on with the next. Start with something they can quickly know when it is healed, if possible, e.g. a pain or discomfort that can be easily identified. "Growing out arms or

legs", "the pelvic thing" or "the neck thing" is almost always a good way to start.

24. Healing the sick takes persistence and practice. Everyone to whom you minister at first may not necessarily be healed, but Jesus promised that we would do the same things He did, and even greater things, and He healed all who came to Him for healing. We believe that eventually all who come to the Spirit-filled believing body of Christ for healing will be healed. The key is to never stop obeying the Great Commission Jesus gave us, Mark 16:15-18.

25. We can call into being those things which are not as though they are (Rom. 4:17). God has a whole warehouse of spare parts. A new tire is better than a retread. Did you ever notice the retreads that "blow" on the highway and have pieces scattered all over the place? Go for a new part. Charles says that I have more new parts than I have originals!

26. Don't let them lose their healing through doubt and unbelief. Stay with them until they actually know that they are healed. The devil comes to steal their

healing, so don't let him. Make sure they continue to praise God.

27. Don't sit on the back burner waiting for God to call you. He has already called you according to Mark 16:15-18, and told you what to do. He said, *"These signs shall follow those who believe...they will lay hands on the sick and they will recover."*

    Beloved, God is doing a new thing. God's message for the hour is for us, ALL of us, as believers, to go out and lay hands on the sick, then God will do His part; they will recover.

28. When Jesus was ministering here on earth, He did not work up emotions, or give long complicated prayers. He simply spoke healing into the person. If you are baptized with the Holy Spirit, then that same power that raised Jesus from the dead flows out of you. It is God's power that touches a person's body and it is His power that does the healing. When you lay hands on someone in Jesus' name, the healing virtue of God flows from the Spirit of God within you to those to whom you are ministering.

29. Since you are filled with the Holy Spirit,

and He is the anointed One, then His anointing power is always in you. So keep in mind that the anointing is not something that comes and goes periodically, but He remains within you.

30 At times the question comes up, can you get people healed if they have doubt and unbelief? The Bible says that signs will follow those who believe. We also know that JESUS HEALED SO THAT PEOPLE WOULD BELIEVE. It is true that unbelief can stop healing, yet often those who are watching when someone gets healed are the first to repent and receive Jesus as Savior.

31. Never forget to use wisdom, common sense, good judgment and discretion. In other words, don't be a "flake."

32. Be careful not to minister on a long-term basis together with someone of the opposite sex, unless it is your wife or husband. As soon as possible find a partner who is the same sex as you are, especially when you are going out to minister in the community.

33. If someone needs healing in a private part of their body, have them put their hand over or near the area, then place

your hand on top of theirs. Be discreet in all you do, for you represent Jesus.

34. Don't allow yourself to become discouraged. The devil loves to come in on the situation and try to cause your faith to go right out your feet. You may find yourself facing a difficult disease the first time you step out. Don't let it throw you. Just remember this, if you are dead to self, then you won't worry about what people say. Just do your best, asking the Holy Spirit to lead you and to speak to you.

35. When ministering to someone who has a sore or an open cut or a discharge, do not place your hand on the affected area directly. Instead have the person place their hand near or over the area, then you place your hand on top of theirs to minister. Of course God's power can prevent spreading disease, but we are in the world and are subject to natural laws of God. After ministering be sure to wash your hands thoroughly. This is just good common hygiene.

36. When ministering to anyone, please find out if they are saved, and if not, minister salvation.

37. Always determine if the person to whom you are ministering has received the baptism with the Holy Spirit and speaks in tongues. If not, then minister to them.
38. Be bold!
39. Having done all, stand! (Eph. 6:13)

Chapter Twelve

Diseases from A to Z

Listed below, in alphabetical order, are many common diseases for which you will be ministering healing and deliverance. Some of these will require the same approach as others, so in our listing, we will simply state what to do. The "how to do it" is covered either in the book, HOW TO HEAL THE SICK, in this book, or in the video/audio tapes, HOW TO HEAL THE SICK.

THE NAME OF JESUS

The name of Jesus is above every other name.

You cannot repeat this too much or too often. Jesus gave us the authority to cast out devils and to minister healing to whatever disease people have. When you speak "In the

name of Jesus" or "In Jesus' name", that
means you are ministering by the authority
Jesus has given to us, the believer.

Jesus told us to use that power and authority to do His works on earth and to destroy the works of the devil.

Remember whatever we bind on earth is
bound in heaven, and whatever we loose on
earth is loosed in heaven.

Common sense and basic knowledge
will lead you to minister in greater detail
than shown herein. Be alert to comments
and answers given by the one to whom you
are ministering.

The Holy Spirit will lead you more specifically as you minister to a person, learning
their needs. Let your very soul reach out in
compassion to meet their needs, whatever
the disease.

Suggested Salvation Prayer

Father, in the name of Jesus, I ask you to
forgive all of my sins. Jesus, come into my
heart and live in me. Thank you, Jesus, for
coming into my heart. Thank you that all my
sins are forgiven and that I have been born
again.

TO CAST OUT A SPIRIT

Say, "Devil (or Satan) I bind you in the name of Jesus, and by the power of God's Holy Spirit, you foul spirit of _____ _____, come out in the name of Jesus!

DISEASE	HOW TO MINISTER

ABUSE

Remember, it is not the child's fault that the abuse occurred, nor is abuse limited to children.

1. Lay hands on their heads, asking God to erase the memories.
2. Speak the peace of God upon them.

ACNE, SEVERE

Multiple skin infections, (pimples, sores), usually caused by overactivity of the sebaceous (oil) glands of the skin.

1. Rebuke (or curse) the infection and command it to go.
2. Cast out the spirit of inheritance.
3. Lay hands on the head commanding the skin pores to open and the sebaceous glands to drain normally.
4. Command the cells that manufacture skin to manufacture normal functioning skin.

ADDICTION:

Alcohol, Cigarette or Drug
Physical and psychological dependence on a substance e.g. alcohol, nicotine in cigarettes, or drugs (e.g. tranquilizers, cocaine, marijuana, heroin etc.)

1. Ask the person if they want to be set free.
2. Ask them if they are saved.
3. Lead the person in the prayer of salvation.
4. Bind and cast out the spirit of alcohol, drug and/or tobacco addiction.
5. Command the body to be healed and the desire for the drugs, tobacco and/or alcohol to be gone.

ADRENAL GLANDS

An endocrine gland located adjacent to the kidneys. Produces hormones and "flight" or "fight" energy necessary to the body.

See also Chapter on "SPINE".

1. "Grow out their Arms" and lay hands over their kidneys commanding the adrenal glands to function properly.
2. Ask if they have any unforgiveness, explaining that anger or other negative emotions cause the adrenal glands to over-secrete adrenalin which can contribute to arthritis, blood pressure or other problems.

"...IN THE NAME OF JESUS."

DISEASE	**HOW TO MINISTER**

ADDISON'S DISEASE - *See also CUSHING'S SYNDROME.*
Failure of the adrenal glands to produce necessary adrenal hormones.

1. Command a creative miracle - a new pair of adrenal glands.
2. Command the hormone levels to be normal.

ADENOIDS, SWOLLEN

1. Place hand on the nose/throat area, commanding the adenoids to shrink and become normal.
2. Do "TNT".

ADHESIONS- *See SCAR TISSUE.*

AGORAPHOBIA
(Panic Attacks)
Severe anxiety causing a fear of going into open places or public areas.

1. Cast out the spirits of fear and anxiety.
2. Speak the peace of God into their heart.
3. Recommend that they fill their mind with the Word of God.
4. Minister salvation and the baptism with the Holy Spirit if applicable.

AIDS - *See Chapter "WHEN MINISTERING HEALING."*

ALLERGIES
Body's negative reaction to a foreign substance. Includes hay fever, drug reactions, food allergies, etc.

See also ASTHMA.

1. Cast out the spirits of inheritance and allergy.
2. Lay hands on the head commanding the immune system to return to normal, all the tissues and organs to be healed and function normally.
3. Do "the total thing".

ALZHEIMER'S DISEASE
A disease of unknown cause that results in deterioration of the brain with memory and reasoning loss.

1. Cast out the spirits of Alzheimer's disease and inheritance.
2. Speak a creative miracle and command a new brain.

"...IN THE NAME OF JESUS."

DISEASE	HOW TO MINISTER

AMBLYOPIA - *see EYES.*

AMYOTROPIC LATERAL SCLEROSIS, ALS

Also known as Lou Gehrig's disease - A degeneration of the nerves of the spinal cord with progressive weakness. Medically irreversible.

1. Bind and cast out the spirit of ALS.
2. Do "TTT" commanding a creative miracle for all new nerves in the spinal cord and body.

ANEMIA

A reduction below normal of red blood cells.

1. Command the bone marrow to be healed and to manufacture normal amounts of healthy red blood cells.

Anemia, Pernicious

Low blood count caused by a failure to absorb vitamin B-12 from the G.I. (gastrointestinal) tract.

1. Command the intestinal tract to be healed and to properly absorb and utilize vitamin B-12.
2. Command the bone marrow to produce rich healthy red blood cells.

ANEURYSM

A condition where the artery wall is thinned and stretched out; possibility of rupture exists. Can occur anywhere in the body.

1. Lay hands on the affected area, commanding a creative miracle - new arteries with good strong walls.
2. Command restoration of normal blood flow.

"...IN THE NAME OF JESUS."

DISEASE	HOW TO MINISTER

ANOREXIA NERVOSA

An eating disorder where the person is practically starving themselves, usually emotionally based.

1. Bind and cast out the spirits of rejection and anorexia.
2. Speak peace and self-confidence to them.
3. Ask if they are saved — have them repeat the prayer of salvation.
4. Explain that our bodies are God's holy temple and we must not do anything to injure ourselves e.g. not eating, self-induced vomiting, etc.
5. Command the "appestat" (the appetite control center in the brain) to be reset for a normal appetite.

"APPESTAT"

The brain's control center for the appetite (or desire for food).

See Chapter THE "APPESTAT"

ARCHES - see FEET.

1. Lay hands on the front and back of the head, commanding the "Appestat" to be healed.
2. Command the metabolism to function normally and person's weight to be within healthy boundaries.

"...IN THE NAME OF JESUS."

DISEASE	HOW TO MINISTER

ARMS AND HANDS
Numbness, Tingling &
Pain - *Usually caused by*
a neck problem.

1. "Grow out their Arms". Do "TNT" commanding the vertebrae and discs to align and the nerves to be restored to normal structure and function.
2. Minister healing to other causes.

ARTERIOSCLEROSIS
"Hardening of the ar-
teries" caused by de-
posits of cholesterol in-
side the arteries (blood
vessels).

1. Do "TNT".
2. Speak a divine "roto-rooter" of God's power to completely clean out all the arteries of all cholesterol plaques.

ARTHRITIS
A painful inflammation
of the joints.

See Chapter "SPINE".

1. Bind and cast out the spirit of arthritis.
2. Command the inflammation to be healed and pain to go.
3. Do "TNT" and "TPT".
4. Mention that most arthritis stems from harbored anger and resentment or unforgiveness. Pray a prayer of forgiveness.

ASTHMA
Condition in the lungs
causing wheezing and
shortness of breath.
Often runs in families
and often associated
with allergies.

1. Cast out the spirit of asthma.
2. Do "TNT".
3. "Grow out the Arms".
4. Speak the peace of God into their life.

ASTIGMATISM - *See EYE.*

"...IN THE NAME OF JESUS."

DISEASE   **HOW TO MINISTER**

AUTISM

Usually describing a child who does not relate to his environment, especially other people, who usually does not talk, yet has nothing physically wrong.

See Chapter "WHEN MINISTERING HEALING"

1. Use extreme gentleness and a quiet attitude; hold them if possible.
2. Speaking softly but firmly, bind and cast out the spirit of autism.
3. While touching them, command the brain to function normally and the total restoration of nervous system.
4. Speak the peace of God into the heart and soul.

"B"

BACK PROBLEMS

1. Determine what to do by finding out what is wrong e.g. what is the doctor's diagnosis? What do you know is wrong specifically, do you have pain? Were you in an accident? Have you had surgery?
2. Do "TNT" - For healing above the waist, "Grow out the Arms." For healing below the waist, "Grow out Legs" and do "TPT."
3. Do any or all of these as needed and repeat if necessary.
4. Command the discs, vertebrae, muscles, ligaments and tendons to be healed and adjusted. Be specific in making the command to the extent you know what is wrong.

"...IN THE NAME OF JESUS."

DISEASE	HOW TO MINISTER

Disc Problems

Commonly called "slipped disc"; disc (or cushion) between two vertebrae (bones in your back) has either deteriorated or is bulging out pressing on a nerve causing discomfort and pain.

1. Do "TTT" (or minister as explained above) commanding the disc to be restored and be healed, recreated if necessary; all pressure on the nerves to be released.
2. Command the vertebrae to be healed, rotated back into place, bones to come together if fractured, ribs be healed and go back into place. Deal with each specific back problem one at a time if you have enough information. Use common sense. Test their healing. Have them put their faith into action.

BALANCE - LOSS OF

1. Ask what their doctor says has caused the problem.
2. Rebuke the cause e.g. infection, disease etc. of the loss of balance.
3. Do "TNT" and "Grow out the Arms" commanding the balance center in the inner ear to be healed and the temporal bones to rotate back into position.

BALDNESS

Inability to grow normal amounts of hair on the head.

1. Command healing to the hair follicles.
2. Command the hair to be restored to normal growth.

BARRENNESS - *See INFERTILITY.*

"...IN THE NAME OF JESUS."

DISEASE	HOW TO MINISTER

BED WETTING

Almost always will have a short leg.

1. "Grow out the Legs" and do "TPT" commanding the vertebrae in the lower back to be adjusted, the nerves to the bladder to be released, the bladder to be healed and function properly.
2. Speak blessings on the child. We normally also whisper a prayer in their ear asking God to station an angel with them to awaken them if they need to go to the bathroom at night so they need not be afraid.

BELL'S PALSY

Damage to the nerve on the side of the face; may be due to a virus infection; normally causes severe pain and paralysis of the facial muscles with a drooping appearance.

1. Cast out the spirit causing Bell's palsy.
2. Command the pain to go.
3. Lay hands gently on the face, commanding the nerves to be regenerated and restored to perfect function.

BIRTH - EASY DELIVERY

1. Ask Jesus to bless the baby in the womb with the power of the Holy Spirit and dedicate the child to God.
2. Ask God to oil the birth canal with the oil of the Holy Spirit and let the baby slide painlessly out within three hours "after" the mother reaches the hospital.

"...IN THE NAME OF JESUS."

DISEASE	HOW TO MINISTER

BLADDER PROBLEMS

Control

Usually caused by damage to structures or nerves

1. Command the bladder and nerve tissues to be healed and restored to normal function.
2. "Grow out the Legs."
3. Do "TPT."

Infections

May be caused by abnormal anatomy especially if frequent infections are occurring.

1. Rebuke the infection.
2. Do "TPT" and "Grow out the Legs" commanding the bladder and all the tissues and nerves to be restored to normal structure and function.

BLINDNESS - *See EYES.*

BLOOD PRESSURE PROBLEMS

Caused by numerous dysfunctions of the body organs. Ask if the doctor has diagnosed any possible underlying causes e.g. diabetes, arteriosclerosis, kidney problems, heart disease etc.

1. Command the heart to be healed, the arteries and vessels to be opened and function normally with proper elasticity. Include other organs if a diagnosis was made involving them also.
2. Do "TNT" and "Grow out the Arms" commanding the muscles and nerves to be normal and allow blood to flow properly.

BOWED LEGS

Knees swing outward giving person a "cowboy" look.

1. Do "TPT" and "Grow out the Legs" commanding the legs to straighten.

BRAIN DAMAGE

1. If caused by a stroke, command the spirit of death of the brain cells to come out.
2. Lay hands on head, commanding a creative miracle - a new brain (brain tissue is not regenerated by the body).
3. Command all the nerves to function normally and any memory loss to be restored.

"...IN THE NAME OF JESUS."

DISEASE	HOW TO MINISTER

BROKEN BONES

1. Lay hands on the affected area commanding the affected bones to come together in normal alignment and strength and be healed.
2. Command all muscles, tendons, nerves and ligaments to line up with the healed bone and strengthen the area previously damaged.

BRONCHITIS

Irritation and inflammation of the bronchial tubes (connects the nose to the lungs).

1. Rebuke the infection.
2. Lay hands on the upper chest and throat commanding the tissues in the bronchial tubes and lungs to be healed and function normally.

BULIMIA

A constant, excessive, insatiable appetite, and often induced vomiting and eating in a repeated cycle.
See Chapter on THE "APPESTAT".

1. Cast out the spirits of bulimia, rejection and anxiety.
2. Do "TNT" commanding the "appestat" to be readjusted to normal.
3. Speak peace, self-confidence and love to the person's spirit and soul

BUNION - *See FEET.*

BURSITIS

Inflammation of fluid-filled sacs that facilitate tendon/muscle movement over bones.

1. Cast out the spirit of bursitis.
2. Touch the affected area and command all inflammation and pain to go, all tissues to be healed and normal fluid be produced for painless movement of the joints.

"...IN THE NAME OF JESUS."

DISEASE	HOW TO MINISTER

CANCER

A tumor which grows progressively through the body. Includes leukemia, lymphoma, and other malignant tumors.

1. Bind and cast out the spirit of cancer.
2. Curse the seed, root and cells of the cancer.
3. Lay hands on the affected area, commanding every cancer cell in the body to die.
4. Command the bone marrow to produce pure healthy blood.
5. Command healing to all organs and tissues affected and restoration of parts where necessary.
6. Command the body's defensive "killer" cells to multiply and attack all cancer cells.

CANDIDA

A fungal (yeast) infection which affects the mucous membranes of the body; generally cause of vaginal infections; aggravated by sugar intake; cause of thrush (a form of candida) in children.

1. Rebuke the infection.
2. Command the body's systems to be restored to normal function.
3. "Grow out the Legs" and do "TPT" commanding nerves and muscles to be relaxed and normal.

CARPAL TUNNEL SYNDROME

A nerve is compressed inside the wrist (carpal tunnel) leading to pain and weakness in the hand.

1. Lay hands on the wrist area and command the tissues, tendons and ligaments in the wrist to be healed and relaxed.
2. Command the "tunnel" to open up and pressure on the nerve to be released, to be healed and to function normally.
3. "Grow out the Arms" and do "TNT" commanding normal circulation and strength to be restored.

"...IN THE NAME OF JESUS."

DISEASE	HOW TO MINISTER

CATARACTS - *See Chapter "EYE HEALINGS"*

CEREBRAL PALSY
1. Cast out the spirit of cerebral palsy.
2. Speak a new brain into body.
3. Do "TTT" - activating the communication from the brain to the other body parts, commanding the muscles, tendons and nerves to function properly.

CHOLESTEROL, HIGH
Too much "fat" in diet.
1. Command the cholesterol level to return to normal and the body to retain only the necessary amounts.
2. Lay hands on their head, commanding all potentially damaged parts of the body to become normal, e.g. arteries, heart.

CLEFT PALATE
An undeveloped roof of the mouth.
1. Cast out the spirit of inheritance.
2. Lay hands on the mouth commanding a creative miracle; all the tissues and structures to be normal.

CIGARETTES - *See ADDICTIONS.*

COLDS - *See INFLUENZA.*

COLD SORES - *See HERPES.*

COLITIS
1. Do "TPT" and "Grow Out Legs", commanding the nerves controlling the colon to be loosed.
2. Command the colon to be healed.

"...IN THE NAME OF JESUS."

DISEASE	HOW TO MINISTER

COMA

Unconsciousness caused by disease or severe trauma.

1. Cast out the spirit of death.
2. Lay hands on the head commanding the brain to be healed; command a creative miracle to any damaged brain tissue (brain tissue will not regenerate).
3. Command the body and all its organs to operate normally and consciousness to return.
4. Speak to the person's soul — their soul is not in a coma. Lead them to Jesus if they are not saved even though they cannot say the prayer, their souls can respond.

CONSTIPATION

Usually caused by dietary problems.

1. Do "TPT" and "Grow out the Legs" commanding the colon to function normally.

CORNS - *See FEET.*

CROHN'S DISEASE

Chronic inflammation of the mucous membranes of the intestinal tract.

1. Cast out the spirit of Crohn's disease.
2. Rebuke the infection.
3. "Grow out the Legs" and do "TPT" commanding the bowel tissue to be healed and function normally.

CUSHING'S SYNDROME

Overactivity of the adrenal glands.

1. Cast out the Cushing's Syndrome spirit.
2. Lay hands on the kidney area of the back, commanding the adrenal glands to function properly.

"...IN THE NAME OF JESUS."

| **DISEASE** | **HOW TO MINISTER** |

CYSTIC DISEASE

Condition affecting women, usually near or at menopause; characterized by rapid development of cysts in a breast. Also called fibrocystic disease or cystic mastitis.

1. Cast out the spirit of fibrocystic disease.
2. Lay hands on chest commanding all the cysts to dissolve and disappear, all the cells and tissues of the breast to be healed and normal, and a creative miracle for any damaged parts.

CYSTIC FIBROSIS

An inherited disease leading to chronic lung disease; most commonly found only in children because usual lifespan of these people is very short; also affects the pancreas and liver.

1. Bind and cast out the spirits of inheritance and cystic fibrosis.
2. Lay hands on the area of the pancreas and liver commanding the glands of the body to secrete normally.
3. Command the lungs, pancreas and liver to be healed and function normally.

"D"

DEAFNESS

May be caused by a deaf spirit attaching itself to the body, an inherited spirit, nerve failure, punctured or damaged ear-drum. Determine by inquiry, if possible, the cause of the deafness and the percent of hearing loss.

1. Cast out the spirit of deafness.
2. Put your fingers gently in the person's ears and command the deafness to go and hearing to be restored.
3. Grow out their arms.
4. Command a new eardrum and bone structures, if needed.
5. Do "TNT" commanding the nerves and muscles to relax, releasing the nerves to the ears, and allowing the blood to flow into the ears, and commanding the hair-like nerves to the inner ear to grow.
6. Place the hands on the sides of the skull and command the temporal bones to rotate back into position. Test their hearing and repeat the above if necessary.

"...IN THE NAME OF JESUS."

DISEASE	HOW TO MINISTER

DEAF MUTE

Person who can neither hear nor speak.

1. Cast out the deaf and dumb spirit.
2. Continue instructions as for DEAF-NESS.
3. Test both hearing and speaking.

DEPRESSION - *See MENTAL ILLNESS*

DERMATITIS

Inflammation of the skin.

1. Rebuke the infection and itching.
2. Command cells which manufacture skin to create new and healthy tissue.

DETACHED RETINA - *See EYES.*

DIABETES

Lack of insulin production by pancreas.

See also HYPOGLYCEMIA.

1. Cast out the spirits of inheritance and diabetes.
2. Command a new pancreas into the body.
3. Command any damaged body parts (from excess sugar) to be healed and made whole.

DIARRHEA

1. Do "TTT".
2. Command digestive system to be healed, and rebuke infection.

DISC DISEASE - *See BACK PROBLEMS.*

DIVERTICULOSIS/ DIVERTICULITIS

Outpouchings (small herniated sacs) of the mucous membrane of the bowel through the muscular wall.

1. Do "TPT" commanding the sacs to disappear and the bowel wall to return to normal strength and function.
2. Command infection to go and tissues totally healed.

See also CROHN'S DISEASE

"...IN THE NAME OF JESUS."

DISEASE   **HOW TO MINISTER**

DOWAGER'S HUMP - *See OSTEOPOROSIS.*

DOWN'S SYNDROME - *See MONGOLISM.*

DROWNING

Excessive fluid into the   1. Bind and cast out the spirit of death.
lungs.   2. Command the water to come out of
                                 the lungs.
                              3. Command life to re-enter the body.
                              4. Command the brain and body to
                                 function normally and be totally
                                 healed.

DYSLEXIA

Impairment of the abil-   1. Command the nerves of the eyes to
ity to read.   function normally and send proper
                                 messages to the brain.
                              2. Command the brain to interpret sig-
                                 nals received and impart under-
                                 standing to the person.

"E"

EARS:

Tinnitus

Abnormal ringing, roar-   1. Cast out the spirit of tinnitus.
ing or hissing.   2. Do "TNT".
                              3. Command the blood to flow through
                                 the ear canal.

Deafness - *See DEAFNESS.*

Fungus or Infection   1. Rebuke the fungus or infection.
                              2. Do "TNT" and command the blood
                                 to flow into the ears and remove im-
                                 purities.

Meniere's Disease   1. Cast out spirit.
                              2. Command ears to be healed and bal-
                                 ance restored.

"...IN THE NAME OF JESUS."

DISEASE	HOW TO MINISTER

ECZEMA
Disease of the skin.

1. Cast out the spirit of eczema.
2. Command the inflammation to go. Curse the infirmity.
3. Command the cells which manufacture skin to replace the damaged tissues and for the skin to return to normal structure, function and texture.

EDEMA
Abnormal collection of fluid in the body. Also called DROPSY.

1. Command healing for any underlying disease.
2. Command the involved organs or tissues be healed and function normally.
3. Command a divine diuretic (cause the fluid to pass through the body).

EMPHYSEMA
Lung disease - inability to breathe properly.

1. Minister deliverance from smoking, if necessary.
2. Minister salvation and baptism of the Holy Spirit, if needed.
3. "Grow out the Arms" commanding a creative miracle — a new set of lungs with healthy lung tissue to function properly.
4. Command other damaged body tissue to become normal.

ENCEPHALITIS
Inflammation of the brain. Usually caused by a viral infection.

1. Rebuke the infection.
2. Command the swelling to go and the brain to be healed, restored and function normally.
3. Do "TNT" commanding the blood to flow normally into the brain.

"...IN THE NAME OF JESUS."

DISEASE	HOW TO MINISTER

ENDOMETRIOSIS

Tumor/tissue in female organs. Pain with the menstrual period.

1. Do "TPT" commanding the female organs to function normally.
2. "Grow out the Legs".
3. Command the extra tissue to dissolve and disappear.

EPILEPSY

Brain problem - seizures.

1. Cast out the spirit of epilepsy. (Jesus did!)
2. Speak a new brain in body.

EYES - *See chapter on "EYE HEALINGS."*

Astigmatism

Abnormal shape of the eye.

1. Command all parts of the eye to be healed and return to normal shape.
2. Do "TNT"

Blindness

Vision damage. Determine, if you can, how much they can see before and after ministering.

1. If the cause is known, address it specifically, e.g. glaucoma, cataracts, infection, detached retina, etc.
2. Bind and cast out the spirit of blindness.
3. Command healing to the eyes and perfect sight to be restored.
4. Do "TNT".
5. Command a creative miracle to the nerves, eye structures and brain.

Cataract

A clouding of the lens of the eye.

1. Lay hands on eyes.
2. Command the blood and fluid to flow through the "onion" layers.

See chapter on "EYE HEALINGS."

"...IN THE NAME OF JESUS."

DISEASE	HOW TO MINISTER

Crossed Eyes
Eyes focus inwards.

Walleyed
Eyes focus outwards.

1. Place your hands over the eyes and command the muscles, ligaments and tissues to be healed and of normal strength and length.
2. Command any scar tissue to be removed.

Detached Retina

1. Lay hands on the eye(s) and command the retina and its nerve endings to reconnect to the eye and be healed.
2. Command the eye to function normally and eyesight to be restored to normal.

Dry Eyes

1. Command any blockage or abnormality to be gone and healing to take place.
2. Command the glands to produce normal amounts of fluid to keep the eyes healthy.

Farsightedness
Inability to see items up close.

1. Lay hands on the eyes commanding the lens, nerves, ligaments and muscles to be adjusted and work properly.
2. Command perfect sight to be restored.

Floaters or "Webbing"

1. Lay hands on the eyes commanding the blood and fluid in the eyes to be restored to normal function and all foreign substances to dissolve and go.
2. Command any scar tissue to be healed.

"...IN THE NAME OF JESUS."

DISEASE	HOW TO MINISTER

Glaucoma
Increased pressure within the eyeball.

1. Command the canals of the eyes to open, pressure to normalize and allow fluid to flow normally.
2. Command any disease process or scar tissue to be healed, and eyes to return to normal.

Lazy Eye

1. Command eye muscles to be of equal length and strength and the nerves to function normally.
2. Command the eye to be healed and vision to be normal.

Macular Degeneration
Retina deterioration.

1. Lay hands over the eyes. Speak a creative miracle and command a new retina.

Nearsightedness
Inability to see far off.
Also known as Myopia.

1. Lay hands on the eyes commanding the lens, nerves, ligaments and muscles to be adjusted and work properly.
2. Command perfect sight to be restored.

Retinitis Pigmentosa
Shrinking of the retina.

1. Lay hands on the eyes commanding a creative miracle to the eye for a new retina and perfect vision.

"...IN THE NAME OF JESUS."

| **DISEASE** | **HOW TO MINISTER** |

FEAR

Abnormal fear of normal situations, people, and/ or things. Ask what they fear.

1. Tell them fear is of the devil and perfect love casts out fear.
2. Cast out the spirit of fear.
3. Speak the peace of God into them and ask God to spiritually erase the fear and any remembrance of previous episodes.
4. Suggest they read a modern version of the Bible at least one hour a day; memorize II Timothy 1:7.
5. Ask God to station a special angel with them.

FEET - *Most foot problems are inherited.*

Arches (Fallen)

1. Do "the pelvic thing" commanding the sacrum and pelvis be adjusted to normal position.
2. Command arches to form.

Bunions

A swelling in the joint of the big toe.

1. Cast out the spirit of inheritance.
2. Rebuke the inflammation.
3. Do "TPT" and/or "Grow out the Legs" commanding the toe and bones to go back into place and the ligaments to strengthen, the foot to be normal.

Callouses and Corns

1. Lay hands on the affected area commanding the corns and callouses to fall off and be replaced by healthy tissue.

Duck Feet

Feet turn excessively outwards.

1. Cast out the spirit of inheritance.
2. Do "TPT" and command the pelvic bones to rotate inward, hips, legs and feet to return to normal position and be totally healed.

"...IN THE NAME OF JESUS."

DISEASE	**HOW TO MINISTER**

Pigeon Toes
Feet turned inwards.

1. Cast out the spirit of inheritance.
2. Do "TPT" and command the pelvic bones to rotate outward and into normal position.

FEMALE PROBLEMS
Any problems with the female reproductive organs of the body. Includes painful menstrual periods, PMS (Premenstrual Syndrome) and prolapsed uterus.

1. "Grow out the legs" and/or do "TPT" commanding all the tissues, nerves and vessels to function normally and sacrum to rotate into correct position.
2. Command any infection or irritation to go.
3. Command all scar tissue, damaged or destroyed parts to be restored and function properly.
4. Command all hormones to be released within the body in normal amounts and a divine diuretic to rid the body of any excess fluid.

Fibroid Tumors
Benign (not cancer) tumors of the uterus.

1. Cast out the spirit causing the tumor.
2. Command the tumor cells to die and dissolve.
3. "Grow out the legs" and/or do "TPT" commanding the tissues of the reproductive organs be restored to normal function and be totally healed.

FISSURE, RECTAL
Crack or tear in the rectum.

1. Tap the cheeks on the face (reflex point) and command the tissues to be healed and fissure to close.

FLU - *See INFLUENZA.*
FUNGUS - *See INFECTIONS.*

"...IN THE NAME OF JESUS."

DISEASE	HOW TO MINISTER

GALL STONES

1. Lay your hand over the area of the gall bladder commanding the stones to dissolve.
2. Command the gall bladder to be healed and function normally.

GANGLION CYST
Hard tumor-like swelling filled with fluid found usually on the wrist around a tendon or joint.

1. Lay hands on the affected area commanding the cyst to dissolve and fluid to re-absorb into the body.
2. Command the wrist structures, bones, muscles and tendons to go back into normal position.
3. Command the joint lining to produce proper joint fluid and blood supply to be normal.
4. Command all pressure on the nerves to go back to normal.

GLAUCOMA - *See EYES.*

GLUTTONY - *See chapter THE "APPESTAT".*

GOITER
Swelling of the thyroid gland.

1. Lay hands on the goiter, and command it to dissolve.
2. Command a new thyroid gland.

GOUT
Deposits of crystals in joints and other organs usually of great toe.

1. Lay hands on the affected foot and command the crystals to dissolve and tissues and bones to be healed.
2. Command the body to metabolize normally.

"...IN THE NAME OF JESUS."

DISEASE	HOW TO MINISTER

GUILLAIN-BARRE/SYNDROME

Nerve deterioration causing paralysis of the body; thought to be caused by viral infection.

1. Rebuke the infection.
2. Lay hands on the person and command the nervous system to be restored and function perfectly.
3. Command any other structures that have been damaged by the paralysis to become whole.
4. Do "TTT".

GUM DISEASE

Diseases of the tissues around the teeth.

1. Rebuke the infection.
2. Lay hands on the jawbone commanding the tissues of the mouth to be healed.

"H"

HAIR - *See BALDNESS.*

HAMMER TOES - *See FEET.*

HANDS - *See ARMS & HANDS.*

HAY FEVER - *See ALLERGIES.*

"...IN THE NAME OF JESUS."

DISEASE	HOW TO MINISTER

HEADACHE

Commonly caused by tension as well as many disease processes e.g. colds, TMJ, infection, tumors, high blood pressure, etc.

1. Do "TNT" commanding the blood to flow normally and spasms of the vessels to release.
2. Cast out the spirit of migraine (if necessary).
3. Instruct the person to move their head and stretch the neck area, then ask, "What happened to the pain?"

HEART

Any problem involving the heart.

1. Speak a new heart into the body.
2. "Grow out the Arms" and do "TNT".
3. Command other body parts that have been affected by the heart disease to be healed.

HEMORRHOIDS

Enlarged blood vessels in the tissues surrounding the rectum.

1. Tap the person's cheeks (the colon reflex area) and command the hemorrhoids to be healed in Jesus' name.
2. Command the blood vessels to shrink to normal size and function.
3. Rebuke pain.

HERNIAS

An outpouching of tissue through an area of weakened muscle.

Hiatus Hernia

Protruding of stomach above the diaphragm leading to pain, indigestion and swallowing difficulties.

1. "Grow out the Arms" commanding all the bones, muscles, nerves and ligaments to be in proper alignment, strengthened, and function.
2. Lay hands on the hernia commanding it to be healed.

"...IN THE NAME OF JESUS."

DISEASE	HOW TO MINISTER

Inguinal, Umbilical or Abdominal

Outpouching of the intestinal tract in the abdomen, inguinal area (where upper thigh meets the lower abdomen), or umbilicus (belly button).

1. "Grow out the Legs".
2. Do "TPT" commanding the hernia to disappear, muscles, tendons, and tissues to be healed and restored to normal strength.

HERPES

A viral infection affecting various parts of the body.

1. Command the infection to go.
2. Command the tissues to be healed and restored to normal.

Herpes Simplex - *Commonly called a "cold sore".*

Herpes Zoster - *Commonly called "shingles".*

Herpes Progenitalis - *"Sores" appear on the external reproductive tissues of the body.*

See also VENEREAL DISEASE

HYPERTENSION (HIGH BLOOD PRESSURE)

Blood pressure which is abnormally high. Ask if cause is known.

See also FEAR

1. Command a divine "roto-rooter" treatment throughout entire vascular system.
2. Command the blood pressure to return to normal and to remain normal.
3. Suggest time in the Word of God every day and to relax in Jesus, eliminating unnecessary tension, anxiety and fear.

"...IN THE NAME OF JESUS."

DISEASE	HOW TO MINISTER

HOMOSEXUALS/LESBIANS

Individuals who prefer intimate relationships with others of the same sex; homosexual refers to males, lesbian refers to females. The individual must want to be free from the desire before they can be delivered and healed from this condition.

See Chapter 7, AIDS

1. Lead the person in the prayer of salvation and total commitment. Say, "Father, I will please You with my lifestyle and not myself."
2. Minister the baptism with the Holy Spirit.
3. Bind and cast out the spirit of homosexuality or lesbianism.
4. Command the desires to be heterosexually (desire for the opposite sex) oriented.

HUNTINGTON'S CHOREA

Hereditary disease characterized by involuntary twisting and writhing movements of the extremities and face, disturbed speech and thinking impairment.

1. Cast out the spirits of inheritance and Huntington's disease.
2. Command a new brain to form.

HYPOGLYCEMIA

Abnormally low blood sugar; sometimes the first indication of early diabetes.

1. Cast out the spirits of inheritance and hypoglycemia.
2. Command a new pancreas to produce normal blood sugar levels.

"I"

INCURABLE DISEASES

Any disease for which doctors cannot find the cure.

1. Cast out the spirit of (whatever disease involved).
2. Speak healing to the body.

"...IN THE NAME OF JESUS."

| DISEASE | HOW TO MINISTER |

INFECTIONS

Caused from numerous organisms e.g. bacteria, virus, fungus or parasite.

1. Rebuke the infection.
2. Command the body to be healed and restored to normal condition and function.
3. Do "TTT".

INFERTILITY

Inability to conceive children.

1. Say, "Father, your Word says the womb of your children shall not be barren and you will make the barren woman the joyful mother of many children. I speak the first one in here, perfect, whole and delivered within one year."
2. Do "TPT."
3. Command any abnormal formations to become normal.

INFLUENZA, FLU, COLDS

1. Rebuke the infection.
2. "Grow out the Arms" and do "TNT" commanding the blood vessels to open and allow the blood to flow freely to free the affected area(s) of germs.
3. Tell them to drink eight glasses of water per day to flush germs from system.
4. Command the intestinal symptoms to go in Jesus' name and that the body accept and utilize food normally.

"...IN THE NAME OF JESUS."

DISEASE	HOW TO MINISTER

INNER HEALING

Healing of memories e.g. hurts, insults, cruel treatment; usually caused by another person.

See Chapter 3, "FALL-ING UNDER THE POWER."

1. Ask God to take His divine spiritual eraser and remove the hurts of the past.
2. Ask the person to forgive anyone who has hurt them.
3. Lay hands on their head and ask Jesus to bless them. Generally, they will go under the power for the Holy Spirit to minister to them.

INSOMNIA

Inability to sleep.

1. Speak the peace and love of God into them. Recommend that the person spend time in the Word of God and possibly listen to a Bible cassette as they go to sleep.
2. Command the sleep center of the brain to operate normally.

"J"

JAW - *See TMJ*

JOINTS: FROZEN or DISLOCATED

See Chapter 8, "THE SPINE."

1. Cast out the spirits of arthritis and bursitis.
2. Do any part of or all the "TTT" as appropriate.
3. Command the joint with its cartilage, ligaments, tendons and tissues to be healed and loosed as you tap the joint lightly with your hand. tell the person to begin to move the extremity.
4. If a bone is out of joint, command it to go back into the socket and stay there.

"...IN THE NAME OF JESUS."

DISEASE	HOW TO MINISTER

KIDNEYS

The organs of the body which remove unnecessary substances from the blood (e.g. fluid, chemicals etc.) and pass them out of the body in the form of urine.

Kidney Damage or Kidney Failure

Does not pass the excess fluid and/or chemicals out of the body causing condition which poisons the body; many underlying causes for damage or failure.

1. Do "TPT" and/or "Grow out the Legs" commanding a new pair of kidneys to operate and function normally.
2. Command healing for underlying causes e.g. disease, high blood pressure, infection, etc.

Kidney Stones

1. Command the stones to dissolve.
2. Command the pain to go.
3. Command the kidneys and all damaged tissues to be healed and restored to normal function.

KNEECAP PROBLEMS - *See LEGS.*

KNOCK-KNEES - *See LEGS.*

"L"

LEGS

KNEECAP PROBLEMS

Can be caused by disease or trauma.

1. If arthritis, cast out the spirit.
2. Lay hands on the affected area commanding all the tendons, ligaments, muscles, cartilage and tissues to be healed; the blood and fluid to lubricate the area to be restored.
3. Command a new kneecap, if needed.
4. "Grow out the Legs·"

"...IN THE NAME OF JESUS."

DISEASE	HOW TO MINISTER

KNOCK-KNEES

1. Do "TPT" commanding the pelvic bone to rotate outward.
2. "Grow out the Legs" commanding the legs and knees to straighten.

LIGAMENTS, TORN OR DAMAGED

Usually caused by twisting or excessive stretching.

1. Rebuke any infection.
2. "Grow out the Arms or Legs" as appropriate.
3. Do "TNT" and "TPT" as appropriate.
4. Command the ligaments to be healed and restored to normal function.

SHORT LEG

Generally caused from a lower back problem which draws up the ligaments, muscles and bones making the leg appear to be "short"; leg bone etc. can actually be permanently shorter because of abnormal development.

1. "Grow out Legs" commanding the back to be healed and muscles and ligaments to go into right position.
2. Do "TPT".
3. If leg is actually shorter or smaller, command a creative miracle - for it to grow to normal length and size.

LEUKEMIA - *See CANCER.*

LOU GEHRIG'S DISEASE - *See AMYOTROPIC LATERAL SCLEROSIS.*

LUMPS

Any abnormal growth in the body.

1. Curse the core, root and cause of the lump.
2. Lay hands on the affected area (or on top of their hands as they touch the area) commanding the lump to dissolve and disappear.
3. Command all tissues to be healed.

"...IN THE NAME OF JESUS."

DISEASE	HOW TO MINISTER

LUNGS - RESPIRATORY RESTRICTIONS

1. Command new lungs, air sacs to open, excess fluid to dry up, or whatever is needed.

LUPUS
Disease when the body attacks itself; can affect many organs in the body including the skin, kidneys and joints.

1. Cast out the spirit of lupus.
2. Command the immune system and all affected organs to be healed and function normally.

"M"

MACULAR DEGENERATION - *See EYES.*

MARRIAGE PROBLEMS

1. Remind them that what they do to each other, they do to Jesus who lives within each of them. Also tell them that their marriage is a practice ground for their marriage to Jesus.
2. Ask if they are both saved and Spirit-filled. If not, minister to them.
3. Lay hands on each of them both at the same time (if present) and speak the peace of God on them and ask God's blessings on their marriage.
4. If only one is present or saved, ask God to station angels around the unsaved member.

MEASLES - *See INFECTION.*

MENIERE'S DISEASE
Disturbance in the inner ear.

Also see EARS.

1. Cast out the spirit of Meniere's disease.
2. Command the inner ear to be healed, the nerves and blood flow to the inner ear to be normal and all dizziness to stop.

"...IN THE NAME OF JESUS."

DISEASE	HOW TO MINISTER

MENTAL ILLNESS
See Chapter 7, "WHEN MINISTERING HEAL-ING."

1. Command spirit to come out.
2. If insanity, cast out the insane spirit.
3. If caused by an accident, command a new brain.
4. If a chemical disorder, command the production of proper chemicals in normal amounts.
5. Lay hands for the Holy Spirit to minister to their needs.

MENSTRUAL PAIN - *See FEMALE PROBLEMS.*

MIGRAINE - *See HEADACHE.*

MONGOLISM, DOWN'S SYNDROME

1. Bind and cast out the spirit of mongolism.
2. Lay hands on their head, command a new brain.
3. Command the cells to revert to the correct number of chromosomes, and for the extra chromosome to go.
4. Command the body to be healed and function normally. Command the facial features to be normal.

MOTION SICKNESS

1. Command the inner ear to adjust to movements.
2. Lay hands on the head, commanding peace to the brain.

MULTIPLE SCLEROSIS, MS

1. Bind and cast out the spirit of MS.
2. Do "TTT" commanding the nerves to be healed and restored to normal structure and function.
3. Command healing and normal function to all parts of the body which have been affected by the disease.

"...IN THE NAME OF JESUS."

DISEASE	HOW TO MINISTER

MUSCULAR DYSTROPHY, MD
Progressive degeneration of muscles.

1. Cast out the spirit of muscular dystrophy.
2. Do "TTT" commanding the muscles to be healed, restored and function normally.

MYASTHENIA GRAVIS
Disease characterized by weakness and rapid tiring of voluntary skeletal muscles.

1. Cast out the spirit of myasthenia gravis.
2. Do "TTT" commanding the nerve receptors on the muscles to be healed and function normally.

"N"

NARCOLEPSY
Uncontrollable episodes of sleep during normal waking hours.

1. Cast out the spirit of narcolepsy.
2. Lay hands on the head, commanding the sleep center of the brain to be healed and to function normally.

NECK
Including muscle strain, pain and/or cracked vertebrae.

1. Do the "TNT".
2. Command vertebrae, discs, muscles, ligaments, nerves, and tendons to be healed and to go back into normal position.

"...IN THE NAME OF JESUS."

DISEASES	HOW TO MINISTER

NERVOUSNESS
See also FEAR and ANXIETY.

1. Cast out the spirits of fear and anxiety
2. Lay hands on their head and speak the peace of God into the mind.

NOSE
Deformed or broken.

1. Lay your finger on the nose and run it down the crest, commanding it to be straight, structures to be regenerated, and function normally.

NUMBNESS
Caused by disease or pinching of the nerves.

1. Command any disease process to go.
2. Do "TTT" commanding discs and vertebrae of the back to return to normal position; pressure on the nerves to be released and nerves to function normally.

"O"

OBESITY
Condition of being excessively overweight.

See Chapter 9, "THE APPESTAT."

1. Lay hands on the head and command the "appestat" (appetite control center) to be readjusted to the normal level and weight to return to correct and healthy range.

OSTEOARTHRITIS - *See ARTHRITIS.*

OSTEOPOROSIS - DOWAGER'S HUMP.
Deterioration of bones.

1. Cast out the spirit of osteoporosis.
2. Do "TTT" commanding the bones to use the calcium and other necessary minerals in the body to regenerate new strong bones.
3. Command the back and sacrum to straighten.

"...IN THE NAME OF JESUS."

DISEASE	HOW TO MINISTER

PALSY - *See PARKINSON'S DISEASE.*

PARKINSON'S DISEASE
Degeneration of cells in the base of the brain accompanied by shaking.

1. Cast out the spirit of Parkinson's disease.
2. Do "TNT" commanding a new brain and nerve tissue that will function normally.
3. Command healing to all other affected parts of the body.

PHLEBITIS
Irritation of blood vessels.

1. Command blood clot to dissolve.
2. Command infection to leave.

PITUITARY GLAND
Endocrine gland located at base of the brain.

1. If cause known, minister to cause.
2. Lay hands on head and/or do "TNT", commanding the pituitary gland to function properly and produce normal amounts of all its hormones.
3. Command all other affected body parts to become normal.

POLIO, POLIOMYELITIS
Infectious virus.

1. Cast out the spirit of polio.
2. Do "TTT" commanding creative miracles to the spinal cord and its damaged nerves, muscles, ligaments, tissues and tendons to be healed, strengthen and function normally.

PMS, PREMENSTRUAL SYNDROME - *See FEMALE PROBLEMS.*

PREGNANCY - *See BIRTH and INFERTILITY.*

PROLAPSED UTERUS - *See FEMALE PROBLEMS.*

"...IN THE NAME OF JESUS."

DISEASE	HOW TO MINISTER

PROSTATE TROUBLE
Enlargement of male re-
productive gland.

1. "Grow out the Legs" and do "TPT" commanding the prostate gland to shrink to normal size and function normally.
2. Command nerves and blood to work normally.

PSORIASIS
Skin disease.

1. Cast out the spirit of psoriasis.
2. Rebuke the inflammation, itching and scaling.
3. Lay hands near (not on) the affected areas commanding healthy new skin cells to replace the affected tissues.

"R"

RESPIRATORY DISEASES - *See LUNGS.*

RETARDATION
Inability to develop or
learn normally; may be
caused by brain damage
or disease.

1. Cast out the spirit of inheritance.
2. Lay hands on the head commanding a new brain with normal intelligence.

RETINITIS PIGMENTOSA - *See EYES.*

RHEUMATIC FEVER

1. Rebuke the infection.
2. Do "TTT" commanding the joints, heart and other tissues of the body to be healed and react normally.
3. Command any damaged organs to be healed and function properly.

RHEUMATOID ARTHRITIS - *See ARTHRITIS.*

In addition to the ministering mentioned under ARTHRITIS, command the immune system to be healed.

RINGING IN THE EARS - *See EARS.*

"...IN THE NAME OF JESUS."

DISEASE	HOW TO MINISTER

SCARS, KELOIDS, ADHESIONS

Keloids - abnormal scars on skin.
Adhesions - abnormal growing together of tissues and/or organs inside the body; usually following surgery.

1. Do whichever of "TTT" relates to the affected area commanding the scar tissue to be dissolved.
2. Command all organs and structures to be healed and function normally.

SCHIZOPHRENIA - *See MENTAL ILLNESS.*

SCIATICA

Pain running along large nerves from spine into thigh.

1. "Grow out the Legs" and do "TPT" commanding the lumbar vertebra and sacrum to be properly aligned.
2. Command all the discs to go back into place and relieve all pressure on the nerves.
3. Place your fingers on either side of the spine above the sacrum and command the sciatica spirit to come out.

SCLERODERMA

Skin feels like it is turning to stone.

1. Cast out the spirit of scleroderma.
2. Do "TTT" commanding the immune system to be healed and return to normal function.
3. Command new tissue to replace the damaged areas of the skin and all affected internal organs.

SCOLIOSIS

Abnormal curvature of the spine.

1. Cast out the spirit of scoliosis.
2. Do "TTT" commanding the bones in the back, the ribs and supportive structures of the body to come into alignment.

"...IN THE NAME OF JESUS."

| **DISEASE** | **HOW TO MINISTER** |

SICKLE-CELL ANEMIA

Hereditary disease usually found in Negroes; red blood cells become "sickle" shaped and clog blood vessels.

1. Cast out the spirit of inheritance.
2. Command the defective genes to be restored to normal and marrow to produce normal blood cells, and the affected organs and tissues of the body to be healed.

SINUS PROBLEMS

1. Rebuke the infection and curse the allergy.
2. Lay hands on the face and command the sinuses to drain, open up and be healed.
3. "Grow out the Arms" commanding blood vessels to open and reduce swelling of the areas.
4. Suggest they avoid irritating factors e.g. sugar, caffeine and nicotine aggravate sinus infection.
5. Drinking eight glasses of water (and juice) daily will alleviate problem also.

SPINA BIFIDA

Birth defect in the spine.

1. Speak a creative miracle into the body. Command spine to close.

STOMACH

Also see ULCERS.

1. Determine specific defect and command it to be healed or new part created.
2. Do "the pelvic thing" and grow out the legs.

"...IN THE NAME OF JESUS."

DISEASE	HOW TO MINISTER

STROKE

Blockage of a blood vessel leading to the brain.

1. Cast out the spirit of death.
2. Lay hands on the head, commanding the blockage to dissolve and be removed; all damaged tissue be restored; a creative miracle - a new brain if necessary.
3. Do "TTT" commanding the communication from the brain to the body and all affected parts of the body be restored to normal function.
4. See detail in HOW TO HEAL THE SICK.

SUICIDE

Taking your own life.

See Chapter 7 on "WHEN MINISTERING HEALING."

1. Bind and cast out the spirit of suicide.
2. Lead them in the prayer of salvation and minister the baptism with the Holy Spirit.
3. Urge them to attend a good church with a Spirit-filled pastor. If possible, make this connection for them.
4. Recommend they spend a lot of time reading a modern version of the Bible, and other good books e.g. POSSESSING THE MIND OF CHRIST by Frances.

"T"

TAILBONE OR COCCYX

Lowest bone of the spinal column.

1. Have the person put their hand on the area and you place your hand over theirs, commanding the tailbone to be healed and to return to its normal position.
2. "Grow out Legs."
3. Command the connective tissues, ligaments and tendons to be healed and the pain to go.
4. Do "TPT."

"...IN THE NAME OF JESUS."

DISEASE	HOW TO MINISTER

TEETH

Crooked

1. Cast out the spirit of inheritance.
2. Lay hands on the jaw, commanding the jaws to be adjusted to allow enough space for the teeth to be in proper alignment.
3. Command the teeth to line up properly.

Decay

1. Curse the decay.
2. Lay hands on the jaw commanding a creative miracle - teeth to be restored and covered with a perfect layer of enamel.

Grinding
Usually occurs at night while asleep. See also TMJ.

1. Do "TNT" and "Grow out the Arms", commanding nerves to be released.
2. Speak the mind of Christ into the person and suggest they spend time in the Bible.
3. If necessary, deal with unforgiveness.

Overbite or Underbite
Caused by jaw being out of place.

See also TMJ.

1. Cast out the spirit of inheritance.
2. Do "TNT" commanding the jaw to be adjusted and moved into right alignment.

TMJ SYNDROME
Inflammation of the "hinge-joint" of the jaw.

1. Do "TTT" commanding the TMJ to go back into place.
2. Command the tissues, ligaments and cartilage to be healed and adjusted to the right alignment.

"...IN THE NAME OF JESUS."

DISEASE	HOW TO MINISTER

TENDONITIS
Inflammation and/or ir-ritation of the tendons.

1. Rebuke the inflammation.
2. Do the appropriate portion of "TTT" (e.g. "Grow out the Arms" for the elbow and shoulder, "Grow out the Legs" for the knee or hip) commanding the tendon and its surrounding tissues to be healed.
3. Command the pain, all swelling and irritation to go.

THYROID DISEASE

1. Do "TNT."
2. Speak a creative miracle - a new thyroid gland.

TIC DOULOUREUX
Severe pain in the side of the face.

1. Cast out the spirit.
2. Do "TNT" commanding the pain to go and the nerve to be healed.

TINNITUS - *See EARS.*

TOES - *See FEET.*

TONSILITIS

1. Rebuke the infection.
2. Do "TNT" commanding the tonsils to shrink to normal size and function normally.

TWITCHING

1. Lay hands on the affected area, commanding all pressure to be relieved, all irritation be gone and the nerves to be healed.

"...IN THE NAME OF JESUS."

DISEASE	HOW TO MINISTER

ULCERS
Open sores in the stomach or small bowel; can also be on skin.

1. Command tissues in the affected area to be healed - a new lining if necessary.
2. Do "TTT" commanding the stomach to produce acid in normal levels.
3. Speak the peace of God into their mind and heart.

UTERUS - *See FEMALE PROBLEMS.*

"V"

VARICOSE VEINS
Veins (usually of the legs) which have become abnormally dilated.

1. Cast out the spirit of inheritance.
2. "Grow out the Legs" commanding the vessel walls to strengthen and function normally, any blockage to be removed and the blood to flow normally back to the heart.

VENEREAL DISEASE
Disease passed through sexual relations. Includes gonorrhea, syphillis, AIDS, some herpes.

1. If the disease was passed during a sinful act, be sure they have repented and promised God they would not repeat the sexual sin again.
2. Minister salvation and the baptism.
3. Rebuke the infection.
4. Cast out the spirit of lust, if appropriate.
5. Lay hands on them, commanding healing to all affected body parts, creative miracles as necessary and the blood to be clean and clear.
6. Command the immune system to be restored to normal for AIDS.

VERTIGO - *See EARS.*

"...IN THE NAME OF JESUS."

DISEASE	HOW TO MINISTER

WARTS

1. Curse the seed and the root of the wart.
2. Command the wart to dry up and fall off.
3. Tell them to touch the warts daily and say, "Thank you, Jesus" until they fall off.

WATER ON THE KNEE OR ELBOW - *See EDEMA.*

WATER RETENTION *See EDEMA.*

WEIGHT LOSS

1. Ask what the doctor considers the cause.
2. Minister to whatever the cause.
3. Command the "appestat" to be readjusted to normal and the body to adjust to a proper weight.

WHIPLASH
Usually the result of a car accident.

1. Do "TTT".
2. Command any damaged disc, vertebrae, nerve, ligament, tendon, or muscles to be healed.

"Z"

Z Z Z - *Lack of insomnia.*

"...IN THE NAME OF JESUS."